LENT 2021 JOURNEY AND MY WAY OF THE CROSS

Catholic Lenten Daily Mass Readings, Practices,
Stations of the Cross and Prayers

CLARK T. SPENCER

Catholic Lectors Press
3299 Elliot Avenue
Seattle, WA 98109
Washington
USA

CONTENTS

iv

LENT

Lent is the time of spiritual preparation prior to the Easter season, just as Advent is for Christmas. Jesus taught us clearly that there is no resurrection without the Cross, and Lent is the Church's great spiritual journey as she, the Bride of Christ, joins her Divine spouse in His great suffering on our behalf. The Lenten season begins on Ash Wednesday and ends approximately six weeks (40 days) later on Holy Thursday, the memorial of the Lord's Supper. The Thursday of Holy Week before Easter Sunday is known as the Holy Thursday. The last week of Lent is Holy Week, starting with Palm Sunday. Following the New Testament story, Jesus' crucifixion is commemorated on Good Friday, and at the beginning of the following week the joyful celebration of Easter Sunday recalls the Resurrection of Jesus Christ.

During Lent, we as Catholics are reminded to devote ourselves to seeking the Lord in prayer, to service by giving alms, and to practice self-control through fasting. Many know of the tradition of abstaining from meat on Fridays during Lent, but we are also called to practice self-discipline and fast in other ways throughout the season. In Lent, the baptized are called to renew their baptismal commitment as others prepare to be baptized through the Rite of Christian Initiation of Adults, a period of learning and discernment for individuals who have declared their desire to become Catholics. The key to fruitful observance of these practices is to recognize our link to baptismal renewal. We are called not just to abstain from sin during Lent, but to true conversion of our hearts and minds as followers of Christ. We also recall those waters in which we were baptized into Christ's death, died to sin and evil, and began new life in Christ.

Lent is traditionally described as lasting for 40 days, in commemoration of the 40 days Jesus spent in the wilderness, according to the Gospels of Matthew, Mark and Luke, before beginning his public ministry, during which he fasted, prayed and endured the temptations of the devil. It is a season of penance to prepare our hearts for Easter, the greatest of all Christian feasts.

IMPORTANT DAYS DURING LENT 2021

- **ASH WEDNESDAY – February 17, 2021**: Commemorates the beginning of Lent. It is a day of reflection and repentance from sin. It also is a holy day when Catholic Christians receive ashes on their foreheads.
- **PALM SUNDAY – March 28, 2021**: The activity of waving palm leaves into the air signifies the last week of the Lenten season. Palm Sunday marks the beginning of the Holy Week. Catholic Christians celebrates Jesus's triumphant entry into Jerusalem.
- **HOLY THURSDAY – April 1, 2021**: Commemorates the washing of the feet and Last Supper of Jesus Christ with the Apostles.
- **GOOD FRIDAY – April 2, 2021**: Commemorates the crucifixion of Jesus and his death at Calvary.
- **EASTER SUNDAY – April 4, 2021**: Celebrates the resurrection of Jesus from the dead and his victory over sin and death.

LENTEN PRACTICES

"The seasons and days of penance in the course of the liturgical year (Lent, and each Friday in memory of the death of the Lord) are intense moments of the Church's penitential practice. These times are particularly appropriate for: spiritual exercises, penitential liturgies, pilgrimages as signs of penance, voluntary self-denial such as fasting and almsgiving, and fraternal sharing (charitable and missionary works)." —Catechism of the Catholic Church, 1438.

- *Fasting and Abstinence*
  Ash Wednesday and Good Friday are obligatory days of fasting and abstinence for Catholics. In addition, Fridays during Lent are

obligatory days of abstinence. The norms on fasting are obligatory for every Catholic from age 18 until age 59, while the norms concerning abstinence from meat are binding upon Catholics aged 14 onwards. When fasting, a person is permitted to eat one full meatless meal per day and two small meatless meals sufficient to maintain strength but do not equal a full meal. Liquids, including milk and fruit juice, are permitted. Private, self-imposed observance of fasting on Lenten weekdays and participation in daily Mass is strongly recommended. The only Catholic Christians that are excused from fast and abstinence outside the age limits are the physically or mentally ill and this includes those individuals suffering from chronic illnesses such as diabetes. Also excluded are pregnant or nursing women. In all cases, common sense should prevail, and ill persons should not further jeopardize their health by fasting.

Fasting is a spiritual feast. It does for the soul what food does for the body. The Bible spells out specific spiritual benefits of fasting. It produces humility (Psalm 69:10). It shows our sorrow for our sins (1 Samuel 7:6). It clears a path to God (Daniel 9:3). It is a means of discerning God's will (Ezra 8:21) and a powerful method of prayer (8:23). It's a mark of true conversion (Joel 2:12).

Fasting helps us to be detached from the things of this world. We fast, not because earthly things are evil, but precisely because they're good. They're God's gifts to us. But they're so good that we sometimes prefer the gifts to the Giver. We practice self-indulgence rather than self-denial. We tend to eat and drink to the point where we forget God. How can we enjoy God's gifts without forgetting the Giver? Fasting is a good way to start. The body wants more than it needs, so we should give it less than it wants.

- *Almsgiving*
  Almsgiving, one of the traditional pillars of Lent is a sign of our care for those in need and an expression of our gratitude for all

3

that God has given to us. Works of charity and the promotion of justice are integral elements of the Christian way of life we began when we were baptized. During Lent, we are reminded to focus more intently on almsgiving, which means making the needs of others our own, especially the needy of our world. They are all around us: children and the old, the sick and the suffering, families and individuals, next-door neighbors and people in lands faraway. Whatever we give should be something of ourselves, something that costs us, as we will receive blessings from God in return. Give generously.

Generosity is not simply giving your excess clothes to a place where poor people might purchase them. It's not even writing a generous check at the time a collection is taken up for a cause that benefits the poor. These are wonderful practices, but generosity is an attitude. It is a sense that no matter how much you have, all that you have is gift, and given to you to be shared. It means that sharing with others in need should be one of your personal priorities. That is quite different from assessing all of your needs first, and then giving away what is left over. A spirit of self-less giving means that one of your needs is to share what you have with others.

Almsgiving is not only for the rich or people who have some extra spending money, but also for those who are poor or are struggling. All of us are called upon to go outside of our own personal needs and help others during this time, especially during this time, because we are always called to do this as Christians. Lent is a wonderful time to practice self-less giving, because it takes practice. It also joins us with Jesus, who gave himself completely, for us.

- *Prayer*

Prayer is our conversation with God. Without prayer, fasting and almsgiving are merely actions we do out of tradition without much meaning. It is through prayer that we find the strength to fast. It is through prayer that we develop a closer, more intimate relationship with God. This relationship makes us so grateful for the blessings he has bestowed upon us, that we eagerly give to those less fortunate than us. We might pray especially for the grace to live out our baptismal promises more fully. We might pray for all those who will celebrate the sacrament of reconciliation with us during Lent that they will be truly renewed in their baptismal commitment.

- ## *Confession (Sacrament of Penance)*

  The Sacrament of Penance is strongly recommended as a penitential practice during the entire Lenten Season. Moreover, Catholics are obliged to confess before receiving Holy Communion during the Easter season. It offers us a great opportunity to confess our sins and obtain absolution from them in order to experience God's boundless mercy. In the Sacrament of Reconciliation (Confession), we encounter Jesus Christ, who after rising from the dead breathed the Holy Spirit on his Apostles — the first priests — and gave them the power to forgive sins in his name (John 20:23).

LENT 2021 DAILY MASS READINGS

First Reading: Joel 2:12-18

Even now, says the LORD, return to me with your whole heart, with fasting, and weeping, and mourning; Rend your hearts, not your garments, and return to the LORD, your God. For gracious and merciful is he, slow to anger, rich in kindness, and relenting in punishment. Perhaps he will again relent and leave behind him a blessing, Offerings and libations for the LORD, your God. Blow the trumpet in Zion! Proclaim a fast, call an assembly; Gather the people, notify the congregation; assemble the elders, gather the children and the infants at the breast; Let the bridegroom quit his room and the bride her chamber. Between the porch and the altar let the priests, the ministers of the LORD, weep, and say, "Spare, O LORD, your people, and make not your heritage a reproach, with the nations ruling over them! Why should they say among the peoples, 'Where is their God?'" Then the LORD was stirred to concern for his land and took pity on his people.

Responsorial Psalm: Psalm 51:3-4, 5-6ab, 12-13, 14 and 17
R. (3a) Be merciful, O Lord, for we have sinned.
Have mercy on me, O God, in your goodness; in the greatness of your compassion wipe out my offense. Thoroughly wash me from my guilt and of my sin cleanse me. **R.**

For I acknowledge my offense, and my sin is before me always: "Against you only have I sinned, and done what is evil in your sight." **R.**

A clean heart create for me, O God, and a steadfast spirit renew within me. Cast me not out from your presence, and your Holy Spirit take not from me. **R.**

Give me back the joy of your salvation, and a willing spirit sustain in me. O Lord, open my lips, and my mouth shall proclaim your praise. **R.**

Second Reading: 2 Corinthians 5:20-6:2

Brothers and sisters: We are ambassadors for Christ, as if God were appealing through us. We implore you on behalf of Christ, be reconciled to God. For our sake he made him to be sin who did not know sin, so that we might become the righteousness of God in him. Working together, then, we appeal to you not to receive the grace of God in vain. For he says: *In an acceptable time I heard you, and on the day of salvation I helped you.* Behold, now is a very acceptable time; behold, now is the day of salvation.

Verse before the Gospel: Psalm 95:8

If today you hear his voice, harden not your hearts.

Gospel: Matthew 6:1-6, 16-18

Jesus said to his disciples: "Take care not to perform righteous deeds in order that people may see them; otherwise, you will have no recompense from your heavenly Father. When you give alms, do not blow a trumpet before you, as the hypocrites do in the synagogues and in the streets to win the praise of others. Amen, I say to you, they have received their reward. But when you give alms, do not let your left hand know what your right is doing, so that your almsgiving may be secret. And your Father who sees in secret will repay you. "When you pray, do not be like the hypocrites, who love to stand and pray in the synagogues and on street corners so that others may see them. Amen, I say to you, they have received their reward. But when you pray, go to your inner room, close the door, and pray to your Father in secret. And your Father who sees in secret will repay you. "When you fast, do not look gloomy like the hypocrites. They neglect their appearance, so that they may appear to others to be fasting. Amen, I say to you, they have received their reward. But when you fast, anoint your head and wash your face, so that you may not appear to be fasting, except to your Father who is hidden. And your Father who sees what is hidden will repay you."

First Reading: Deuteronomy 30:15-20

Moses said to the people: "Today I have set before you life and prosperity, death and doom. If you obey the commandments of the LORD, your God, which I enjoin on you today, loving him, and walking in his ways, and keeping his commandments, statutes and decrees, you will live and grow numerous, and the LORD, your God, will bless you in the land you are entering to occupy. If, however, you turn away your hearts and will not listen, but are led astray and adore and serve other gods, I tell you now that you will certainly perish; you will not have a long life on the land that you are crossing the Jordan to enter and occupy. I call heaven and earth today to witness against you: I have set before you life and death, the blessing and the curse. Choose life, then, that you and your descendants may live, by loving the LORD, your God, heeding his voice, and holding fast to him. For that will mean life for you, a long life for you to live on the land that the LORD swore he would give to your fathers Abraham, Isaac and Jacob."

Responsorial Psalm: Psalm 1:1-2, 3, 4 and 6
R. (40:5a) Blessed are they who hope in the Lord.

Blessed the man who follows not the counsel of the wicked nor walks in the way of sinners, nor sits in the company of the insolent, but delights in the law of the LORD and meditates on his law day and night. **R.**

He is like a tree planted near running water, that yields its fruit in due season, and whose leaves never fade. Whatever he does, prospers. **R.**

Not so the wicked, not so; they are like chaff which the wind drives away. For the LORD watches over the way of the just, but the way of the wicked vanishes. **R.**

Verse before the Gospel: Matthew 4:17

Repent, says the Lord; the Kingdom of heaven is at hand.

Gospel: Luke 9:22-25

Jesus said to his disciples: "The Son of Man must suffer greatly and be rejected by the elders, the chief priests, and the scribes, and be killed and on the third day be raised." Then he said to all, "If anyone wishes to come after me, he must deny himself and take up his cross daily and follow me. For whoever wishes to save his life will lose it, but whoever loses his life for my sake will save it. What profit is there for one to gain the whole world yet lose or forfeit himself?"

FRIDAY, FEBRUARY 19
FRIDAY AFTER ASH WEDNESDAY
First Reading: Isaiah 58:1-9a

Thus says the Lord GOD: Cry out full-throated and unsparingly, lift up your voice like a trumpet blast; Tell my people their wickedness, and the house of Jacob their sins. They seek me day after day, and desire to know my ways, like a nation that has done what is just and not abandoned the law of their God; they ask me to declare what is due them, pleased to gain access to God. "Why do we fast, and you do not see it? Afflict ourselves, and you take no note of it?" Lo, on your fast day you carry out your own pursuits, and drive all your laborers. Yes, your fast ends in quarreling and fighting, striking with wicked claw. Would that today you might fast so as to make your voice heard on high! Is this the manner of fasting I wish, of keeping a day of penance: That a man bow his head like a reed and lie in sackcloth and ashes? Do you call this a fast, a day acceptable to the LORD? This, rather, is the fasting that I wish: releasing those bound unjustly, untying the thongs of the yoke; Setting free the oppressed, breaking every yoke; Sharing your bread with the hungry, sheltering the oppressed and the homeless; Clothing the naked when you see them, and not turning your back on your own. Then your light shall break forth like the dawn, and your wound shall quickly be healed; your vindication shall go before you, and the glory of the LORD shall be your rear guard. Then you shall call, and the LORD will answer, you shall cry for help, and he will say: Here I am!

Responsorial Psalm: Psalm 51:3-4, 5-6ab, 18-19

R. (19b) A heart contrite and humbled, O God, you will not spurn.

Have mercy on me, O God, in your goodness; in the greatness of your compassion wipe out my offense. Thoroughly wash me from my guilt and of my sin cleanse me. **R.**

For I acknowledge my offense, and my sin is before me always: "Against you only have I sinned, and done what is evil in your sight." **R.**

For you are not pleased with sacrifices; should I offer a burnt offering, you would not accept it. My sacrifice, O God, is a contrite spirit; a heart contrite and humbled, O God, you will not spurn. **R.**

Verse before the Gospel: Amos 5:14

Seek good and not evil so that you may live, and the Lord will be with you.

Gospel: Matthew 9:14-15

The disciples of John approached Jesus and said, "Why do we and the Pharisees fast much, but your disciples do not fast?" Jesus answered them, "Can the wedding guests mourn as long as the bridegroom is with them? The days will come when the bridegroom is taken away from them, and then they will fast."

SATURDAY, FEBRUARY 20

SATURDAY AFTER ASH WEDNESDAY

First Reading: Isaiah 58:9b-14

Thus says the LORD: If you remove from your midst oppression, false accusation and malicious speech; If you bestow your bread on the hungry and satisfy the afflicted; Then light shall rise for you in the darkness, and the gloom shall become for you like midday; Then the

LORD will guide you always and give you plenty even on the parched land. He will renew your strength, and you shall be like a watered garden, like a spring whose water never fails. The ancient ruins shall be rebuilt for your sake, and the foundations from ages past you shall raise up; "Repairer of the breach," they shall call you, "Restorer of ruined homesteads." If you hold back your foot on the Sabbath from following your own pursuits on my holy day; If you call the Sabbath a delight, and the LORD's holy day honorable; If you honor it by not following your ways, seeking your own interests, or speaking with malice Then you shall delight in the LORD, and I will make you ride on the heights of the earth; I will nourish you with the heritage of Jacob, your father, for the mouth of the LORD has spoken.

Responsorial Psalm: Psalm 86:1-2, 3-4, 5-6
R. (11ab) Teach me your way, O Lord, that I may walk in your truth.

Incline your ear, O LORD; answer me, for I am afflicted and poor. Keep my life, for I am devoted to you; save your servant who trusts in you. You are my God. **R.**

Have mercy on me, O Lord, for to you I call all the day. Gladden the soul of your servant, for to you, O Lord, I lift up my soul. **R.**

For you, O Lord, are good and forgiving, abounding in kindness to all who call upon you. Hearken, O LORD, to my prayer and attend to the sound of my pleading. **R.**

Verse before the Gospel: Ezekiel 33:11
I take no pleasure in the death of the wicked man, says the Lord, but rather in his conversion, that he may live.

Gospel: Luke 5:27-32
Jesus saw a tax collector named Levi sitting at the customs post. He said to him, "Follow me." And leaving everything behind, he got up and followed him. Then Levi gave a great banquet for him in his

11

house, and a large crowd of tax collectors and others were at table with them. The Pharisees and their scribes complained to his disciples, saying, "Why do you eat and drink with tax collectors and sinners?" Jesus said to them in reply, "Those who are healthy do not need a physician, but the sick do. I have not come to call the righteous to repentance but sinners."

First Reading: Genesis 9:8-15

God said to Noah and to his sons with him: "See, I am now establishing my covenant with you and your descendants after you and with every living creature that was with you: all the birds, and the various tame and wild animals that were with you and came out of the ark. I will establish my covenant with you, that never again shall all bodily creatures be destroyed by the waters of a flood; there shall not be another flood to devastate the earth." God added: "This is the sign that I am giving for all ages to come, of the covenant between me and you and every living creature with you: I set my bow in the clouds to serve as a sign of the covenant between me and the earth. When I bring clouds over the earth, and the bow appears in the clouds, I will recall the covenant I have made between me and you and all living beings, so that the waters shall never again become a flood to destroy all mortal beings."

Responsorial Psalm: Psalm 25:4-5, 6-7, 8-9

R. (10) Your ways, O Lord, are love and truth to those who keep your covenant.

Your ways, O LORD, make known to me; teach me your paths, Guide me in your truth and teach me, for you are God my savior. **R.**

Remember that your compassion, O LORD, and your love are from of old. In your kindness remember me, because of your goodness, O LORD. **R.**

Good and upright is the LORD, thus he shows sinners the way. He guides the humble to justice, and he teaches the humble his wa.

Second Reading: 1 Peter 3:18-22

Beloved: Christ suffered for sins once, the righteous for the sake of the unrighteous, that he might lead you to God. Put to death in the flesh, he was brought to life in the Spirit. In it he also went to preach to the spirits in prison, who had once been disobedient while God patiently waited in the days of Noah during the building of the ark, in which a few persons, eight in all, were saved through water. This prefigured baptism, which saves you now. It is not a removal of dirt from the body but an appeal to God for a clear conscience, through the resurrection of Jesus Christ, who has gone into heaven and is at the right hand of God, with angels, authorities, and powers subject to him.

Verse before the Gospel: Matthew 4:4b

One does not live on bread alone, but on every word that comes forth from the mouth of God.

Gospel: Mark 1:12-15

The Spirit drove Jesus out into the desert, and he remained in the desert for forty days, tempted by Satan. He was among wild beasts, and the angels ministered to him. After John had been arrested, Jesus came to Galilee proclaiming the gospel of God: "This is the time of fulfillment. The kingdom of God is at hand. Repent, and believe in the gospel."

MONDAY, FEBRUARY 22
FEAST OF THE CHAIR OF SAINT PETER, APOSTLE
First Reading: 1 Peter 5:1-4

Beloved: I exhort the presbyters among you, as a fellow presbyter and witness to the sufferings of Christ and one who has a share in the glory to be revealed. Tend the flock of God in your midst, overseeing not by constraint but willingly, as God would have it, not for shameful profit but eagerly. Do not lord it over those assigned to you, but be examples to the flock. And when the chief Shepherd is revealed, you will receive the unfading crown of glory.

Responsorial Psalm: Psalm 23:1-3a, 4, 5, 6
R. (1) The Lord is my shepherd; there is nothing I shall want.

The Lord is my shepherd; I shall not want. In verdant pastures he gives me repose; beside restful waters he leads me; he refreshes my soul. **R.**

Even though I walk in the dark valley I fear no evil; for you are at my side with your rod and your staff that give me courage. **R.**

You spread the table before me in the sight of my foes; you anoint my head with oil; my cup overflows. **R.**

Only goodness and kindness follow me all the days of my life; and I shall dwell in the house of the Lord for years to come. **R.**

Alleluia: Matthew 16:18
R. Alleluia, alleluia.

You are Peter, and upon this rock I will build my Church; the gates of the netherworld shall not prevail against it. **R.**

Gospel: Matthew 16:13-19
When Jesus went into the region of Caesarea Philippi he asked his disciples, "Who do people say that the Son of Man is?" They replied, "Some say John the Baptist, others Elijah, still others Jeremiah or one of the prophets." He said to them, "But who do you say that I am?" Simon Peter said in reply, "You are the Christ, the Son of the living God." Jesus said to him in reply, "Blessed are you, Simon son of Jonah. For flesh and blood has not revealed this to you, but my heavenly Father. And so I say to you, you are Peter, and upon this rock I will build my Church, and the gates of the netherworld shall not prevail against it. I will give you the keys to the Kingdom of heaven. Whatever you bind on earth shall be bound in heaven; and whatever you loose on earth shall be loosed in heaven."

First Reading: Isaiah 55:10-11

Thus says the LORD: Just as from the heavens the rain and snow come down And do not return there till they have watered the earth, making it fertile and fruitful, Giving seed to the one who sows and bread to the one who eats, So shall my word be that goes forth from my mouth; It shall not return to me void, but shall do my will, achieving the end for which I sent it.

Responsorial Psalm: Psalm 34:4-5, 6-7, 16-17, 18-19

R. (18b) From all their distress God rescues the just.

Glorify the LORD with me, let us together extol his name. I sought the LORD, and he answered me and delivered me from all my fears. **R**.

Look to him that you may be radiant with joy, and your faces may not blush with shame. When the poor one called out, the LORD heard, and from all his distress he saved him. **R**.

The LORD has eyes for the just, and ears for their cry. The LORD confronts the evildoers, to destroy remembrance of them from the earth. **R**.

When the just cry out, the LORD hears them, and from all their distress he rescues them. The LORD is close to the brokenhearted; and those who are crushed in spirit he saves. **R**.

Verse before the Gospel: Matthew 4:4b

One does not live on bread alone, but on every word that comes forth from the mouth of God.

Gospel: Matthew 6:7-15

Jesus said to his disciples: "In praying, do not babble like the pagans, who think that they will be heard because of their many words. Do not be like them. Your Father knows what you need before you ask him. "This is how you are to pray: Our Father who art in heaven, hallowed be thy name, thy Kingdom come, thy will be done, on earth as it is in heaven. Give us this day our daily bread; and forgive us our trespasses, as we forgive those who trespass against us; and lead us not into temptation, but deliver us from evil. "If you forgive men their transgressions, your heavenly Father will forgive you. But if you do not forgive men, neither will your Father forgive your transgressions."

WEDNESDAY, FEBRUARY 24
WEDNESDAY OF THE FIRST WEEK IN LENT

First Reading: Jonah 3:1-10

The word of the LORD came to Jonah a second time: "Set out for the great city of Nineveh, and announce to it the message that I will tell you." So Jonah made ready and went to Nineveh, according to the LORD's bidding. Now Nineveh was an enormously large city; it took three days to go through it. Jonah began his journey through the city, and had gone but a single day's walk announcing, "Forty days more and Nineveh shall be destroyed," when the people of Nineveh believed God; they proclaimed a fast and all of them, great and small, put on sackcloth. When the news reached the king of Nineveh, he rose from his throne, laid aside his robe, covered himself with sackcloth, and sat in the ashes. Then he had this proclaimed throughout Nineveh, by decree of the king and his nobles: "Neither man nor beast, neither cattle nor sheep, shall taste anything; they shall not eat, nor shall they drink water. Man and beast shall be covered with sackcloth and call loudly to God; every man shall turn from his evil way and from the violence he has in hand. Who knows, God may relent and forgive, and withhold his blazing wrath, so that we shall not perish." When God saw by their actions how they turned from their evil way, he repented of the evil that he had threatened to do to them; he did not carry it out.

Responsorial Psalm: Psalm 51:3-4, 12-13, 18-19

R. (19b) A heart contrite and humbled, O God, you will not spurn.

Have mercy on me, O God, in your goodness; in the greatness of your compassion wipe out my offense. Thoroughly wash me from my guilt and of my sin cleanse me. **R.**

A clean heart create for me, O God, and a steadfast spirit renew within me. Cast me not out from your presence, and your Holy Spirit take not from me. **R.**

For you are not pleased with sacrifices; should I offer a burnt offering, you would not accept it. My sacrifice, O God, is a contrite spirit; a heart contrite and humbled, O God, you will not spurn. **R.**

Verse before the Gospel: Joel 2:12-13

Even now, says the LORD, return to me with your whole heart for I am gracious and merciful.

Gospel: Luke 11:29-32

While still more people gathered in the crowd, Jesus said to them, "This generation is an evil generation; it seeks a sign, but no sign will be given it, except the sign of Jonah. Just as Jonah became a sign to the Ninevites, so will the Son of Man be to this generation. At the judgment the queen of the south will rise with the men of this generation and she will condemn them, because she came from the ends of the earth to hear the wisdom of Solomon, and there is something greater than Solomon here. At the judgment the men of Nineveh will arise with this generation and condemn it, because at the preaching of Jonah they repented, and there is something greater than Jonah here."

THURSDAY, FEBRUARY 25
THURSDAY OF THE FIRST WEEK IN LENT
First Reading: Esther C:12, 14-16, 23-25

Queen Esther, seized with mortal anguish, had recourse to the LORD. She lay prostrate upon the ground, together with her handmaids, from morning until evening, and said: "God of Abraham, God of Isaac, and God of Jacob, blessed are you. Help me, who am alone and have no help but you, for I am taking my life in my hand. As a child I used to hear from the books of my forefathers that you, O LORD, always free those who are pleasing to you. Now help me, who am alone and have no one but you, O LORD, my God. "And now, come to help me, an orphan. Put in my mouth persuasive words in the presence of the lion and turn his heart to hatred for our enemy, so that he and those who are in league with him may perish. Save us from the hand of our enemies; turn our mourning into gladness and our sorrows into wholeness."

Responsorial Psalm: Psalm 138:1-2ab, 2cde-3, 7c-8
R. (3a) Lord, on the day I called for help, you answered me.
I will give thanks to you, O LORD, with all my heart, for you have heard the words of my mouth; in the presence of the angels I will sing your praise; I will worship at your holy temple and give thanks to your name. **R.**
Because of your kindness and your truth; for you have made great above all things your name and your promise. When I called, you answered me; you built up strength within me. **R.**
Your right hand saves me. The LORD will complete what he has done for me; your kindness, O LORD, endures forever; forsake not the work of your hands. **R.**

Verse before the Gospel: Psalm 51:12a, 14a
A clean heart create for me, O God; give me back the joy of your salvation.

Gospel: Matthew 7:7-12
Jesus said to his disciples: "Ask and it will be given to you; seek and you will find; knock and the door will be opened to you. For everyone who asks, receives; and the one who seeks, finds; and to the one who knocks, the door will be opened. Which one of you would

hand his son a stone when he asked for a loaf of bread, or a snake when he asked for a fish? If you then, who are wicked, know how to give good gifts to your children, how much more will your heavenly Father give good things to those who ask him. "Do to others whatever you would have them do to you. This is the law and the prophets."

FRIDAY OF THE FIRST WEEK OF LENT

First Reading: Ezekiel 18:21-28

Thus says the Lord GOD: If the wicked man turns away from all the sins he committed, if he keeps all my statutes and does what is right and just, he shall surely live, he shall not die. None of the crimes he committed shall be remembered against him; he shall live because of the virtue he has practiced. Do I indeed derive any pleasure from the death of the wicked? says the Lord GOD. Do I not rather rejoice when he turns from his evil way that he may live? And if the virtuous man turns from the path of virtue to do evil, the same kind of abominable things that the wicked man does, can he do this and still live? None of his virtuous deeds shall be remembered, because he has broken faith and committed sin; because of this, he shall die. You say, "The LORD's way is not fair!" Hear now, house of Israel: Is it my way that is unfair, or rather, are not your ways unfair? When someone virtuous turns away from virtue to commit iniquity, and dies, it is because of the iniquity he committed that he must die. But if the wicked, turning from the wickedness he has committed, does what is right and just, he shall preserve his life; since he has turned away from all the sins that he committed, he shall surely live, he shall not die.

Responsorial Psalm: Psalm 130:1-2, 3-4, 5-7a, 7bc-8
R. (3) If you, O Lord, mark iniquities, who can stand?

Out of the depths I cry to you, O LORD; LORD, hear my voice! Let your ears be attentive to my voice in supplication. **R.**

If you, O LORD, mark iniquities, LORD, who can stand? But with you is forgiveness, that you may be revered. **R.**

I trust in the LORD; my soul trusts in his word. My soul waits for the LORD more than sentinels wait for the dawn. Let Israel wait for the LORD. **R.**

For with the LORD is kindness and with him is plenteous redemption; and he will redeem Israel from all their iniquities. **R.**

Verse before the Gospel: Ezekiel 18:31

Cast away from you all the crimes you have committed, says the LORD, and make for yourselves a new heart and a new spirit.

Gospel: Matthew 5:20-26

Jesus said to his disciples: "I tell you, unless your righteousness surpasses that of the scribes and Pharisees, you will not enter into the Kingdom of heaven. "You have heard that it was said to your ancestors, *you shall not kill; and whoever kills will be liable to judgment.* But I say to you, whoever is angry with his brother will be liable to judgment, and whoever says to his brother, *Raqa*, will be answerable to the Sanhedrin, and whoever says, 'You fool,' will be liable to fiery Gehenna. Therefore, if you bring your gift to the altar, and there recall that your brother has anything against you, leave your gift there at the altar, go first and be reconciled with your brother, and then come and offer your gift. Settle with your opponent quickly while on the way to court. Otherwise your opponent will hand you over to the judge, and the judge will hand you over to the guard, and you will be thrown into prison. Amen, I say to you, you will not be released until you have paid the last penny."

SATURDAY, FEBRUARY 27
SATURDAY OF THE FIRST WEEK OF LENT

First Reading: Deuteronomy 26:16-19

Moses spoke to the people, saying: "This day the LORD, your God, commands you to observe these statutes and decrees. Be careful, then, to observe them with all your heart and with all your soul. Today you are making this agreement with the LORD: he is to be your God and you are to walk in his ways and observe his statutes, commandments and decrees, and to hearken to his voice. And today the LORD is making this agreement with you: you are to be a people peculiarly his own, as he promised you; and provided you keep all his commandments, he will then raise you high in praise and renown and glory above all other nations he has made, and you will be a people sacred to the LORD, your God, as he promised."

Responsorial Psalm: Psalm 119:1-2, 4-5, 7-8
R. (1b) Blessed are they who follow the law of the Lord!
Blessed are they whose way is blameless, who walk in the law of the LORD. Blessed are they who observe his decrees, who seek him with all their heart. **R.**

You have commanded that your precepts be diligently kept. Oh, that I might be firm in the ways of keeping your statutes! **R.**

I will give you thanks with an upright heart, when I have learned your just ordinances. I will keep your statutes; do not utterly forsake me. **R.**

Verse before the Gospel: 2 Corinthians 6:2b
Behold, now is a very acceptable time; behold, now is the day of salvation.

Gospel: Matthew 5:43-48
Jesus said to his disciples: "You have heard that it was said, *you shall love your neighbor and hate your enemy.* But I say to you, love your enemies, and pray for those who persecute you, that you may be children of your heavenly Father, for he makes his sun rise on the bad and the good, and causes rain to fall on the just and the unjust. For if you love those who love you, what recompense will you have? Do not the tax collectors do the same? And if you greet your brothers and sisters only, what is unusual about that? Do not the

pagans do the same? So be perfect, just as your heavenly Father is perfect."

First Reading: Genesis 22:1-2, 9a, 10-13, 15-18

God put Abraham to the test. He called to him, "Abraham!" "Here I am!" he replied. Then God said: "Take your son Isaac, your only one, whom you love, and go to the land of Moriah. There you shall offer him up as a holocaust on a height that I will point out to you." When they came to the place of which God had told him, Abraham built an altar there and arranged the wood on it. Then he reached out and took the knife to slaughter his son. But the LORD's messenger called to him from heaven, "Abraham, Abraham!" "Here I am!" he answered. "Do not lay your hand on the boy," said the messenger. "Do not do the least thing to him. I know now how devoted you are to God, since you did not withhold from me your own beloved son." As Abraham looked about, he spied a ram caught by its horns in the thicket. So he went and took the ram and offered it up as a holocaust in place of his son. Again the LORD's messenger called to Abraham from heaven and said: "I swear by myself, declares the LORD, that because you acted as you did in not withholding from me your beloved son, I will bless you abundantly and make your descendants as countless as the stars of the sky and the sands of the seashore; your descendants shall take possession of the gates of their enemies, and in your descendants all the nations of the earth shall find blessing— all this because you obeyed my command."

Responsorial Psalm: Psalm 116:10, 15, 16-17, 18-19
R. (116:9) I will walk before the Lord, in the land of the living.
I believed, even when I said, "I am greatly afflicted." Precious in the eyes of the LORD is the death of his faithful ones. **R.**
O LORD, I am your servant; I am your servant, the son of your handmaid; you have loosed my bonds. To you will I offer sacrifice of

thanksgiving, and I will call upon the name of the LORD. **R**.

My vows to the LORD I will pay in the presence of all his people, in the courts of the house of the LORD, in your midst, O Jerusalem. **R**.

Second Reading: Romans 8:31b-34

Brothers and sisters: If God is for us, who can be against us? He who did not spare his own Son but handed him over for us all, how will he not also give us everything else along with him? Who will bring a charge against God's chosen ones? It is God who acquits us, who will condemn? Christ Jesus it is who died—or, rather, was raised— who also is at the right hand of God, who indeed intercedes for us.

Verse before the Gospel: Matthew 17:5

From the shining cloud the Father's voice is heard: This is my beloved Son, listen to him.

Gospel: Mark 9:2-10

Jesus took Peter, James, and John and led them up a high mountain apart by themselves. And he was transfigured before them, and his clothes became dazzling white, such as no fuller on earth could bleach them. Then Elijah appeared to them along with Moses, and they were conversing with Jesus. Then Peter said to Jesus in reply, "Rabbi, it is good that we are here! Let us make three tents: one for you, one for Moses, and one for Elijah." He hardly knew what to say, they were so terrified. Then a cloud came, casting a shadow over them; from the cloud came a voice, "This is my beloved Son. Listen to him." Suddenly, looking around, they no longer saw anyone but Jesus alone with them. As they were coming down from the mountain, he charged them not to relate what they had seen to anyone, except when the Son of Man had risen from the dead. So they kept the matter to themselves, questioning what rising from the dead meant.

First Reading: Daniel 9:4b-10

"Lord, great and awesome God, you who keep your merciful covenant toward those who love you and observe your commandments! We have sinned, been wicked and done evil; we have rebelled and departed from your commandments and your laws. We have not obeyed your servants the prophets, who spoke in your name to our kings, our princes, our fathers, and all the people of the land. Justice, O Lord, is on your side; we are shamefaced even to this day: we, the men of Judah, the residents of Jerusalem, and all Israel, near and far, in all the countries to which you have scattered them because of their treachery toward you. O LORD, we are shamefaced, like our kings, our princes, and our fathers, for having sinned against you. But yours, O Lord, our God, are compassion and forgiveness! Yet we rebelled against you and paid no heed to your command, O LORD, our God, to live by the law you gave us through your servants the prophets."

Responsorial Psalm: Psalm 79:8, 9, 11 and 13
R. (103:10a) Lord, do not deal with us according to our sins.

Remember not against us the iniquities of the past; may your compassion quickly come to us, for we are brought very low. **R.**

Help us, O God our savior, because of the glory of your name; Deliver us and pardon our sins for your name's sake. **R.**

Let the prisoners' sighing come before you; with your great power free those doomed to death. Then we, your people and the sheep of your pasture, will give thanks to you forever; through all generations we will declare your praise. **R.**

Verse before the Gospel: 2 Corinthians 6:2b

Your words, Lord, are Spirit and life; you have the words of everlasting life.

Gospel: John 6:63c, 68c

Jesus said to his disciples: "Be merciful, just as your Father is merciful. "Stop judging and you will not be judged. Stop condemning and you will not be condemned. Forgive and you will be forgiven. Give and gifts will be given to you; a good measure, packed together, shaken down, and overflowing, will be poured into your lap. For the measure with which you measure will in return be measured out to you."

TUESDAY, MARCH 2
TUESDAY OF THE SECOND WEEK OF LENT

First Reading: Isaiah 1:10, 16-20

Hear the word of the LORD, princes of Sodom! Listen to the instruction of our God, people of Gomorrah! Wash yourselves clean! Put away your misdeeds from before my eyes; cease doing evil; learn to do good. Make justice your aim: redress the wronged, hear the orphan's plea, defend the widow. Come now, let us set things right, says the LORD: Though your sins be like scarlet, they may become white as snow; though they be crimson red, they may become white as wool. If you are willing, and obey, you shall eat the good things of the land; but if you refuse and resist, the sword shall consume you: for the mouth of the LORD has spoken!

Responsorial Psalm: Psalm 50:8-9, 16bc-17, 21 and 23
R. (23b) To the upright I will show the saving power of God.

"Not for your sacrifices do I rebuke you, for your burnt offerings are before me always. I take from your house no bullock, no goats out of your fold." **R.**

"Why do you recite my statutes, and profess my covenant with your mouth, though you hate discipline and cast my words behind you?" **R.**

"When you do these things, shall I be deaf to it? Or do you think that I am like yourself? I will correct you by drawing them up before your eyes. He that offers praise as a sacrifice glorifies me; and to him that goes the right way I will show the salvation of God." **R**.

Verse before the Gospel: Ezekiel 18:31
Cast away from you all the crimes you have committed, says the LORD, and make for yourselves a new heart and a new spirit.

Gospel: Matthew 23:1-12
Jesus spoke to the crowds and to his disciples, saying, "The scribes and the Pharisees have taken their seat on the chair of Moses. Therefore, do and observe all things whatsoever they tell you, but do not follow their example. For they preach but they do not practice. They tie up heavy burdens hard to carry and lay them on people's shoulders, but they will not lift a finger to move them. All their works are performed to be seen. They widen their phylacteries and lengthen their tassels. They love places of honor at banquets, seats of honor in synagogues, greetings in marketplaces, and the salutation 'Rabbi.' As for you, do not be called 'Rabbi.' You have but one teacher, and you are all brothers. Call no one on earth your father; you have but one Father in heaven. Do not be called 'Master'; you have but one master, the Christ. The greatest among you must be your servant. Whoever exalts himself will be humbled; but whoever humbles himself will be exalted."

WEDNESDAY, MARCH 3
WEDNESDAY OF THE SECOND WEEK OF LENT
First Reading: Jeremiah 18:18-20
The people of Judah and the citizens of Jerusalem said, "Come, let us contrive a plot against Jeremiah. It will not mean the loss of instruction from the priests, nor of counsel from the wise, nor of messages from the prophets. And so, let us destroy him by his own tongue; let us carefully note his every word." Heed me, O LORD, and listen to what my adversaries say. Must good be repaid with evil that they should dig a pit to take my life? Remember that I stood before you to speak in their behalf, to turn away your wrath from

them.

Responsorial Psalm: Psalm 31:5-6, 14, 15-16
R. (17b) Save me, O Lord, in your kindness.
You will free me from the snare they set for me, for you are my refuge. Into your hands I commend my spirit; you will redeem me, O LORD, O faithful God. **R.**

I hear the whispers of the crowd, that frighten me from every side, as they consult together against me, plotting to take my life. **R.**

But my trust is in you, O LORD; I say, "You are my God." In your hands is my destiny; rescue me from the clutches of my enemies and my persecutors. **R.**

Verse before the Gospel: John 8:12
I am the light of the world, says the Lord; whoever follows me will have the light of life.

Gospel: Matthew 20:17-28
As Jesus was going up to Jerusalem, he took the Twelve disciples aside by themselves, and said to them on the way, "Behold, we are going up to Jerusalem, and the Son of Man will be handed over to the chief priests and the scribes, and they will condemn him to death, and hand him over to the Gentiles to be mocked and scourged and crucified, and he will be raised on the third day." Then the mother of the sons of Zebedee approached Jesus with her sons and did him homage, wishing to ask him for something. He said to her, "What do you wish?" She answered him, "Command that these two sons of mine sit, one at your right and the other at your left, in your kingdom." Jesus said in reply, "You do not know what you are asking. Can you drink the chalice that I am going to drink?" They said to him, "We can." He replied, "My chalice you will indeed drink, but to sit at my right and at my left, this is not mine to give but is for those for whom it has been prepared by my Father." When the ten heard this, they became indignant at the two brothers. But Jesus

summoned them and said, "You know that the rulers of the Gentiles lord it over them, and the great ones make their authority over them felt. But it shall not be so among you. Rather, whoever wishes to be great among you shall be your servant; whoever wishes to be first among you shall be your slave. Just so, the Son of Man did not come to be served but to serve and to give his life as a ransom for many."

THURSDAY, MARCH 4
THURSDAY OF THE SECOND WEEK OF LENT

First Reading: Jeremiah 17:5-10

Thus says the LORD: Cursed is the man who trusts in human beings, who seeks his strength in flesh, whose heart turns away from the LORD. He is like a barren bush in the desert that enjoys no change of season, but stands in a lava waste, a salt and empty earth. Blessed is the man who trusts in the LORD, whose hope is the LORD. He is like a tree planted beside the waters that stretches out its roots to the stream: It fears not the heat when it comes, its leaves stay green; in the year of drought it shows no distress, but still bears fruit. More tortuous than all else is the human heart, beyond remedy; who can understand it? I, the LORD, alone probe the mind and test the heart, to reward everyone according to his ways, according to the merit of his deeds.

Responsorial Psalm: Psalm 1:1-2, 3, 4 and 6
R. (40:5a) Blessed are they who hope in the Lord.

Blessed the man who follows not the counsel of the wicked nor walks in the way of sinners, nor sits in the company of the insolent, but delights in the law of the LORD and meditates on his law day and night. **R.**

He is like a tree planted near running water, that yields its fruit in due season, and whose leaves never fade. Whatever he does, prospers. **R.**

Not so, the wicked, not so; they are like chaff which the wind drives away. For the LORD watches over the way of the just, but the way of the wicked vanishes. **R.**

Verse before the Gospel: Luke 8:15

Blessed are they who have kept the word with a generous heart and yield a harvest through perseverance.

Gospel: Luke 16:19-31

Jesus said to the Pharisees: "There was a rich man who dressed in purple garments and fine linen and dined sumptuously each day. And lying at his door was a poor man named Lazarus, covered with sores, who would gladly have eaten his fill of the scraps that fell from the rich man's table. Dogs even used to come and lick his sores. When the poor man died, he was carried away by angels to the bosom of Abraham. The rich man also died and was buried, and from the netherworld, where he was in torment, he raised his eyes and saw Abraham far off and Lazarus at his side. And he cried out, 'Father Abraham, have pity on me. Send Lazarus to dip the tip of his finger in water and cool my tongue, for I am suffering torment in these flames.' Abraham replied, 'My child, remember that you received what was good during your lifetime while Lazarus likewise received what was bad; but now he is comforted here, whereas you are tormented. Moreover, between us and you a great chasm is established to prevent anyone from crossing who might wish to go from our side to yours or from your side to ours.' He said, 'Then I beg you, father, send him to my father's house, for I have five brothers, so that he may warn them, lest they too come to this place of torment.' But Abraham replied, 'They have Moses and the prophets. Let them listen to them.' He said, 'Oh no, father Abraham, but if someone from the dead goes to them, they will repent.' Then Abraham said, 'If they will not listen to Moses and the prophets, neither will they be persuaded if someone should rise from the dead.'"

FRIDAY, MARCH 5
FRIDAY OF THE SECOND WEEK IN LENT

First Reading: Genesis 37:3-4, 12-13a, 17b-28a

Israel loved Joseph best of all his sons, for he was the child of his old age; and he had made him a long tunic. When his brothers saw that their father loved him best of all his sons, they hated him so much that they would not even greet him. One day, when his brothers had gone to pasture their father's flocks at Shechem, Israel said to Joseph, "Your brothers, you know, are tending our flocks at Shechem. Get ready; I will send you to them." So Joseph went after his brothers and caught up with them in Dothan. They noticed him from a distance, and before he came up to them, they plotted to kill him. They said to one another: "Here comes that master dreamer! Come on, let us kill him and throw him into one of the cisterns here; we could say that a wild beast devoured him. We shall then see what comes of his dreams." When Reuben heard this, he tried to save him from their hands, saying, "We must not take his life. Instead of shedding blood," he continued, "just throw him into that cistern there in the desert; but do not kill him outright." His purpose was to rescue him from their hands and return him to his father. So when Joseph came up to them, they stripped him of the long tunic he had on; then they took him and threw him into the cistern, which was empty and dry. They then sat down to their meal. Looking up, they saw a caravan of Ishmaelites coming from Gilead, their camels laden with gum, balm and resin to be taken down to Egypt. Judah said to his brothers: "What is to be gained by killing our brother and concealing his blood? Rather, let us sell him to these Ishmaelites, instead of doing away with him ourselves. After all, he is our brother, our own flesh." His brothers agreed. They sold Joseph to the Ishmaelites for twenty pieces of silver.

Responsorial Psalm: Psalm 105:16-17, 18-19, 20-21
R. (5a) Remember the marvels the Lord has done.

When the LORD called down a famine on the land and ruined the crop that sustained them, He sent a man before them, Joseph, sold as a slave. **R.**

They had weighed him down with fetters, and he was bound with chains, till his prediction came to pass and the word of the LORD proved him true. **R.**

The king sent and released him, the ruler of the peoples set him free. He made him lord of his house and ruler of all his possessions. **R.**

Verse before the Gospel: John 3:16

God so loved the world that he gave his only-begotten Son; so that everyone who believes in him might have eternal life.

Gospel: Matthew 21:33-43, 45-46

Jesus said to the chief priests and the elders of the people: "Hear another parable. There was a landowner who planted a vineyard, put a hedge around it, dug a wine press in it, and built a tower. Then he leased it to tenants and went on a journey. When vintage time drew near, he sent his servants to the tenants to obtain his produce. But the tenants seized the servants and one they beat, another they killed, and a third they stoned. Again he sent other servants, more numerous than the first ones, but they treated them in the same way. Finally, he sent his son to them, thinking, 'They will respect my son.' But when the tenants saw the son, they said to one another, 'This is the heir. Come, let us kill him and acquire his inheritance.' They seized him, threw him out of the vineyard, and killed him. What will the owner of the vineyard do to those tenants when he comes?" They answered him, He will put those wretched men to a wretched death and lease his vineyard to other tenants who will give him the produce at the proper times." Jesus said to them, did you never read in the Scriptures: *The stone that the builders rejected has become the cornerstone; by the Lord has this been done, and it is wonderful in our eyes?* Therefore, I say to you, the Kingdom of God will be taken away from you and given to a people that will produce its fruit." When the chief priests and the Pharisees heard his parables, they knew that he was speaking about them. And although they were attempting to arrest him, they feared the crowds, for they regarded him as a prophet.

First Reading: Micah 7:14-15, 18-20

Shepherd your people with your staff, the flock of your inheritance, that dwells apart in a woodland, in the midst of Carmel. Let them feed in Bashan and Gilead, as in the days of old; As in the days when you came from the land of Egypt, show us wonderful signs. Who is there like you, the God who removes guilt and pardons sin for the remnant of his inheritance; Who does not persist in anger forever, but delights rather in clemency, And will again have compassion on us, treading underfoot our guilt? You will cast into the depths of the sea all our sins; you will show faithfulness to Jacob, and grace to Abraham, as you have sworn to our fathers from days of old.

Responsorial Psalm: Psalm 103:1-2, 3-4, 9-10, 11-12
R. (8a) The Lord is kind and merciful.

Bless the LORD, O my soul; and all my being, bless his holy name. Bless the LORD, O my soul, and forget not all his benefits. **R.**

He pardons all your iniquities, he heals all your ills. He redeems your life from destruction, he crowns you with kindness and compassion. **R.**

He will not always chide, nor does he keep his wrath forever. Not according to our sins does he deal with us, nor does he requite us according to our crimes. **R.**

For as the heavens are high above the earth, so surpassing is his kindness toward those who fear him. As far as the east is from the west, so far has he put our transgressions from us. **R.**

Verse before the Gospel: Luke 15:18

I will get up and go to my father and shall say to him, Father, I have sinned against heaven and against you.

Gospel: Luke 15:1-3, 11-32

Tax collectors and sinners were all drawing near to listen to Jesus, but the Pharisees and scribes began to complain, saying, "This man welcomes sinners and eats with them." So to them Jesus addressed this parable. "A man had two sons, and the younger son said to his father, 'Father, give me the share of your estate that should come to me.' So the father divided the property between them. After a few days, the younger son collected all his belongings and set off to a distant country where he squandered his inheritance on a life of dissipation. When he had freely spent everything, a severe famine struck that country, and he found himself in dire need. So he hired himself out to one of the local citizens who sent him to his farm to tend the swine. And he longed to eat his fill of the pods on which the swine fed, but nobody gave him any. Coming to his senses he thought, 'How many of my father's hired workers have more than enough food to eat, but here am I, dying from hunger. I shall get up and go to my father and I shall say to him, "Father, I have sinned against heaven and against you. I no longer deserve to be called your son; treat me as you would treat one of your hired workers."' So he got up and went back to his father. While he was still a long way off, his father caught sight of him, and was filled with compassion. He ran to his son, embraced him and kissed him. His son said to him, 'Father, I have sinned against heaven and against you; I no longer deserve to be called your son.' But his father ordered his servants, 'Quickly, bring the finest robe and put it on him; put a ring on his finger and sandals on his feet. Take the fattened calf and slaughter it. Then let us celebrate with a feast, because this son of mine was dead, and has come to life again; he was lost, and has been found.' Then the celebration began. Now the older son had been out in the field and, on his way back, as he neared the house, he heard the sound of music and dancing. He called one of the servants and asked what this might mean. The servant said to him, 'Your brother has returned and your father has slaughtered the fattened calf because he has him back safe and sound.' He became angry, and when he refused to enter the house, his father came out and pleaded with him. He said to his father in reply, 'Look, all these years I served you and not once did I disobey your orders; yet you never gave me even a young goat to feast on with my friends. But when your son returns who swallowed up your property with prostitutes, for him you slaughter the fattened calf.' He said to him, 'My son, you are here with me always; everything I have is yours. But now we must celebrate and rejoice, because your brother was dead and has come to life again; he was lost and has been found.'"

SUNDAY, MARCH 7
THIRD SUNDAY OF LENT
First Reading: Exodus 20:1-17 or 20:1-3, 7-8, 12-17

In those days, God delivered all these commandments: "I, the LORD, am your God, who brought you out of the land of Egypt, that place of slavery. You shall not have other gods besides me. You shall not carve idols for yourselves in the shape of anything in the sky above or on the earth below or in the waters beneath the earth; you shall not bow down before them or worship them. For I, the LORD, your God, am a jealous God, inflicting punishment for their fathers' wickedness on the children of those who hate me, down to the third and fourth generation; but bestowing mercy down to the thousandth generation on the children of those who love me and keep my commandments.

"You shall not take the name of the LORD, your God, in vain. For the LORD will not leave unpunished the one who takes his name in vain.

"Remember to keep holy the Sabbath day. Six days you may labor and do all your work, but the seventh day is the Sabbath of the LORD, your God. No work may be done then either by you, or your son or daughter, or your male or female slave, or your beast, or by the alien who lives with you. In six days the Lord made the heavens and the earth, the sea and all that is in them; but on the seventh day he rested. That is why the LORD has blessed the Sabbath day and made it holy.

"Honor your father and your mother, that you may have a long life in the land which the LORD, your God, is giving you.
You shall not kill.
You shall not commit adultery.
You shall not steal.
You shall not bear false witness against your neighbor.
You shall not covet your neighbor's house.
You shall not covet your neighbor's wife, nor his male or female slave, nor his ox or ass, nor anything else that belongs to him."

Or:
Exodus 20:1-3, 7-8, 12-17
In those days, God delivered all these commandments:
"I, the LORD am your God, who brought you out of the land of Egypt, that place of slavery. You shall not have other gods besides me.
"You shall not take the name of the LORD, your God, in vain. For the LORD will not leave unpunished the one who takes his name in vain.
"Remember to keep holy the Sabbath day.
Honor your father and your mother, that you may have a long life in the land which the Lord, your God, is giving you.
You shall not kill.
You shall not commit adultery.
You shall not steal.
You shall not bear false witness against your neighbor.
You shall not covet your neighbor's house.
You shall not covet your neighbor's wife, nor his male or female slave, nor his ox or ass, nor anything else that belongs to him."

Responsorial Psalm: Psalm 19:8, 9, 10, 11
R. (John 6:68c) Lord, you have the words of everlasting life.
The law of the LORD is perfect, refreshing the soul; the decree of the LORD is trustworthy, giving wisdom to the simple. **R.**

The precepts of the LORD are right, rejoicing the heart; the command of the LORD is clear, enlightening the eye. **R**.

The fear of the LORD is pure, enduring forever; the ordinances of the LORD are true, all of them just. **R**.

They are more precious than gold, than a heap of purest gold; sweeter also than syrup or honey from the comb. **R**.

Second Reading: 1 Corinthians 1:22-25

Brothers and sisters: Jews demand signs and Greeks look for wisdom, but we proclaim Christ crucified, a stumbling block to Jews and foolishness to Gentiles, but to those who are called, Jews and Greeks alike, Christ the power of God and the wisdom of God. For the foolishness of God is wiser than human wisdom, and the weakness of God is stronger than human strength.

Verse before the Gospel: John 3:16

God so loved the world that he gave his only Son, so that everyone who believes in him might have eternal life.

Gospel: John 2:13-25

Since the Passover of the Jews was near, Jesus went up to Jerusalem. He found in the temple area those who sold oxen, sheep, and doves, as well as the money changers seated there. He made a whip out of cords and drove them all out of the temple area, with the sheep and oxen, and spilled the coins of the money changers and overturned their tables, and to those who sold doves he said, "Take these out of here, and stop making my Father's house a marketplace." His disciples recalled the words of Scripture, *Zeal for your house will consume me*. At this the Jews answered and said to him, "What sign can you show us for doing this?" Jesus answered and said to them, "Destroy this temple and in three days I will raise it up." The Jews said, "This temple has been under construction for forty-six years, and you will raise it up in three days?" But he was speaking about the temple of his body. Therefore, when he was raised from the dead, his disciples remembered that he had said this, and they came to believe the Scripture and the word Jesus had spoken. While he was in Jerusalem for the feast of Passover, many began to believe in his name when they saw the signs he was doing. But Jesus would not trust himself to them because he knew them all, and did not need anyone to testify about human nature. He himself understood it well.

MONDAY, MARCH 8
MONDAY OF THE THIRD WEEK OF LENT
First Reading: 2 Kings 5:1-15ab

Naaman, the army commander of the king of Aram, was highly esteemed and respected by his master, for through him the LORD had brought victory to Aram. But valiant as he was, the man was a leper. Now the Arameans had captured in a raid on the land of Israel a little girl, who became the servant of Naaman's wife. "If only my master would present himself to the prophet in Samaria," she said to her mistress, "he would cure him of his leprosy." Naaman went and told his lord just what the slave girl from the land of Israel had said. "Go," said the king of Aram. "I will send along a letter to the king of Israel." So Naaman set out, taking along ten silver talents, six thousand gold pieces, and ten festal garments. To the king of Israel he brought the letter, which read: "With this letter I am sending my servant Naaman to you, that you may cure him of his leprosy." When he read the letter, the king of Israel tore his garments and exclaimed: "Am I a god with power over life and death, that this man should send someone to me to be cured of leprosy? Take note! You can see he is only looking for a quarrel with me!" When Elisha, the man of God, heard that the king of Israel had torn his garments, he sent word to the king: "Why have you torn your garments? Let him come to me and find out that there is a prophet in Israel." Naaman came with his horses and chariots and stopped at the door of Elisha's house. The prophet sent him the message: "Go and wash seven times in the Jordan, and your flesh will heal, and you will be clean." But Naaman went away angry, saying, "I thought that he would surely come out and stand there to invoke the LORD his God, and would move his hand over the spot, and thus cure the leprosy. Are not the rivers of Damascus, the Abana and the Pharpar, better than all the waters of Israel? Could I not wash in them and be cleansed?" With this, he turned about in anger and left. But his servants came up and reasoned with him. "My father," they said, "if the prophet had told you to do something extraordinary, would you not have done it? All the more now, since he said to you, 'Wash and be clean,' should you do as he said." So Naaman went down and plunged into the Jordan seven times at the word of the man of God. His flesh became again like the flesh of a little child, and he was clean. He returned with his whole retinue to the man of God. On his arrival he stood before him and said, "Now I know that there is no God in all the earth, except in Israel."

Responsorial Psalm: Psalm 42:2, 3; 43:3, 4
R. (42:3) Athirst is my soul for the living God. When shall I go and behold the face of God?
As the hind longs for the running waters, so my soul longs for you, O God. **R.**
Athirst is my soul for God, the living God. When shall I go and behold the face of God? **R.**
Send forth your light and your fidelity; they shall lead me on and bring me to your holy mountain, to your dwelling-place. **R.**
Then will I go in to the altar of God, the God of my gladness and joy; then will I give you thanks upon the harp, O God, my God! **R.**

Verse before the Gospel: Psalm 130:5, 7
I hope in the LORD, I trust in his word; with him there is kindness and plenteous redemption.

Gospel: Luke 4:24-30
Jesus said to the people in the synagogue at Nazareth: "Amen, I say to you, no prophet is accepted in his own native place. Indeed, I tell

you, there were many widows in Israel in the days of Elijah when the sky was closed for three and a half years and a severe famine spread over the entire land. It was to none of these that Elijah was sent, but only to a widow in Zarephath in the land of Sidon. Again, there were many lepers in Israel during the time of Elisha the prophet; yet not one of them was cleansed, but only Naaman the Syrian." When the people in the synagogue heard this, they were all filled with fury. They rose up, drove him out of the town, and led him to the brow of the hill on which their town had been built, to hurl him down headlong. But he passed through the midst of them and went away.

TUESDAY, MARCH 9
TUESDAY OF THE THIRD WEEK OF LENT
First Reading: Daniel 3:25, 34-43

Azariah stood up in the fire and prayed aloud: "For your name's sake, O Lord, do not deliver us up forever, or make void your covenant. Do not take away your mercy from us, for the sake of Abraham, your beloved, Isaac your servant, and Israel your holy one, to whom you promised to multiply their offspring like the stars of heaven, or the sand on the shore of the sea. For we are reduced, O Lord, beyond any other nation, brought low everywhere in the world this day because of our sins. We have in our day no prince, prophet, or leader, no burnt offering, sacrifice, oblation, or incense, no place to offer first fruits, to find favor with you. But with contrite heart and humble spirit let us be received; As though it were burnt offerings of rams and bullocks, or thousands of fat lambs, so let our sacrifice be in your presence today as we follow you unreservedly; for those who trust in you cannot be put to shame. And now we follow you with our whole heart, we fear you and we pray to you. Do not let us be put to shame, but deal with us in your kindness and great mercy. Deliver us by your wonders, and bring glory to your name, O Lord."

Responsorial Psalm: Psalm 25:4-5ab, 6 and 7bc, 8-9
R. (6a) Remember your mercies, O Lord.

Your ways, O LORD, make known to me; teach me your paths, guide me in your truth and teach me, for you are God my savior. **R.**

Remember that your compassion, O LORD, and your kindness are from of old. In your kindness remember me, because of your goodness, O LORD. **R.**

Good and upright is the LORD; thus he shows sinners the way. He guides the humble to justice, he teaches the humble his way. **R.**

Verse before the Gospel: Joel 2:12-13

Even now, says the LORD, return to me with your whole heart; for I am gracious and merciful.

Gospel: Matthew 18:21-35

Peter approached Jesus and asked him, "Lord, if my brother sins against me, how often must I forgive him? As many as seven times?" Jesus answered, "I say to you, not seven times but seventy-seven times. That is why the Kingdom of heaven may be likened to a king who decided to settle accounts with his servants. When he began the accounting, a debtor was brought before him who owed him a huge amount. Since he had no way of paying it back, his master ordered him to be sold, along with his wife, his children, and all his property, in payment of the debt. At that, the servant fell down, did him homage, and said, 'Be patient with me, and I will pay you back in full.' Moved with compassion the master of that servant let him go and forgave him the loan. When that servant had left, he found one of his fellow servants who owed him a much smaller amount. He seized him and started to choke him, demanding, 'pay back what you owe.' Falling to his knees, his fellow servant begged him, 'Be patient with me, and I will pay you back.' But he refused. Instead, he had him put in prison until he paid back the debt. Now when his fellow servants saw what had happened, they were deeply disturbed, and went to their master and reported the whole affair. His master summoned him and said to him, 'You wicked servant! I forgave you your entire debt because you begged me to. Should you not have had pity on your fellow servant, as I had pity on you?' Then in anger his master handed him over to the torturers until he should pay back the whole debt. So will my heavenly Father do to you, unless each of you forgives your brother from your heart."

WEDNESDAY, MARCH 10
WEDNESDAY OF THE THIRD WEEK OF LENT
First Reading: Deuteronomy 4:1, 5-9

Moses spoke to the people and said: "Now, Israel, hear the statutes and decrees which I am teaching you to observe, that you may live, and may enter in and take possession of the land which the LORD, the God of your fathers, is giving you. Therefore, I teach you the statutes and decrees as the LORD, my God, has commanded me, that you may observe them in the land you are entering to occupy. Observe them carefully, for thus will you give evidence of your wisdom and intelligence to the nations, who will hear of all these statutes and say, 'This great nation is truly a wise and intelligent people.' For what great nation is there that has gods so close to it as the LORD, our God, is to us whenever we call upon him? Or what great nation has statutes and decrees that are as just as this whole law which I am setting before you today? "However, take care and be earnestly on your guard not to forget the things which your own eyes have seen, nor let them slip from your memory as long as you live, but teach them to your children and to your children's children."

Responsorial Psalm: Psalm 147:12-13, 15-16, 19-20
R. (12a) Praise the Lord, Jerusalem.

Glorify the LORD, O Jerusalem; praise your God, O Zion. For he has strengthened the bars of your gates; he has blessed your children within you. **R**.

He sends forth his command to the earth; swiftly runs his word! He spreads snow like wool; frost he strews like ashes. **R**.

He has proclaimed his word to Jacob, his statutes and his ordinances to Israel. He has not done thus for any other nation; his ordinances he has not made known to them. **R.**

Verse before the Gospel: John 6:63c, 68c

Your words, Lord, are Spirit and life; you have the words of everlasting life.

Gospel: Matthew 5:17-19

Jesus said to his disciples: "Do not think that I have come to abolish the law or the prophets. I have come not to abolish but to fulfill. Amen, I say to you, until heaven and earth pass away, not the smallest letter or the smallest part of a letter will pass from the law, until all things have taken place. Therefore, whoever breaks one of the least of these commandments and teaches others to do so will be called least in the Kingdom of heaven. But whoever obeys and teaches these commandments will be called greatest in the Kingdom of heaven."

THURSDAY, MARCH 11
THURSDAY OF THE THIRD WEEK OF LENT

First Reading: Jeremiah 7:23-28

Thus says the LORD: This is what I commanded my people: Listen to my voice; then I will be your God and you shall be my people. Walk in all the ways that I command you, so that you may prosper. But they obeyed not, nor did they pay heed. They walked in the hardness of their evil hearts and turned their backs, not their faces, to me. From the day that your fathers left the land of Egypt even to this day, I have sent you untiringly all my servants the prophets. Yet they have not obeyed me nor paid heed; they have stiffened their necks and done worse than their fathers. When you speak all these words to them, they will not listen to you either; when you call to them, they will not answer you. Say to them: This is the nation that does not listen to the voice of the LORD, its God, or take correction. Faithfulness has disappeared; the word itself is banished from their speech.

Responsorial Psalm: Psalm 95:1-2, 6-7, 8-9

R. (8) If today you hear his voice, harden not your hearts.

Come, let us sing joyfully to the LORD; let us acclaim the Rock of our salvation. Let us come into his presence with thanksgiving; let us joyfully sing psalms to him. **R.**

Come, let us bow down in worship; let us kneel before the LORD who made us. For he is our God, and we are the people he shepherds, the flock he guides. **R.**

Oh, that today you would hear his voice: "Harden not your hearts as at Meribah, as in the day of Massah in the desert, Where your fathers tempted me; they tested me though they had seen my works." **R.**

Verse before the Gospel: Joel 2:12-13

Even now, says the LORD, return to me with your whole heart, for I am gracious and merciful.

Gospel: Luke 11:14-23

Jesus was driving out a demon that was mute, and when the demon had gone out, the mute man spoke and the crowds were amazed. Some of them said, "By the power of Beelzebul, the prince of demons, he drives out demons." Others, to test him, asked him for a sign from heaven. But he knew their thoughts and said to them, "Every kingdom divided against itself will be laid waste and house will fall against house. And if Satan is divided against himself, how will his kingdom stand? For you say that it is by Beelzebul that I drive out demons. If I, then, drive out demons by Beelzebul, by whom do your own people drive them out? Therefore they will be your judges. But if it is by the finger of God that I drive out demons, then the Kingdom of God has come upon you. When a strong man fully armed guards his palace, his possessions are safe. But when one stronger than he attacks and overcomes him, he takes away the armor on which he relied and distributes the spoils. Whoever is not with me is against me, and whoever does not gather with me scatters."

FRIDAY OF THE THIRD WEEK OF LENT

First Reading: Hosea 14:2-10

Thus says the LORD: Return, O Israel, to the LORD, your God; you have collapsed through your guilt. Take with you words, and return to the LORD; Say to him, "Forgive all iniquity, and receive what is good, that we may render as offerings the bullocks from our stalls. Assyria will not save us, nor shall we have horses to mount; we shall say no more, 'Our god,' to the work of our hands; for in you the orphan finds compassion." I will heal their defection, says the LORD, I will love them freely; for my wrath is turned away from them. I will be like the dew for Israel: he shall blossom like the lily; He shall strike root like the Lebanon cedar, and put forth his shoots. His splendor shall be like the olive tree and his fragrance like the Lebanon cedar. Again they shall dwell in his shade and raise grain; they shall blossom like the vine, and his fame shall be like the wine of Lebanon. Ephraim! What more has he to do with idols? I have humbled him, but I will prosper him. "I am like a verdant cypress tree"– Because of me you bear fruit! Let him who is wise understand these things; let him who is prudent know them. Straight are the paths of the LORD, in them the just walk, but sinners stumble in them.

Responsorial Psalm: Psalm 81:6c-8a, 8bc-9, 10-11ab, 14 and 17
R. (11 and 9a) I am the Lord your God: hear my voice.

An unfamiliar speech I hear: "I relieved his shoulder of the burden; his hands were freed from the basket. In distress you called, and I rescued you." **R.**

"Unseen, I answered you in thunder; I tested you at the waters of Meribah. Hear, my people, and I will admonish you; O Israel, will you not hear me?" **R.**

"There shall be no strange god among you nor shall you worship any alien god. I, the LORD, am your God who led you forth from the land of Egypt." **R.**

"If only my people would hear me, and Israel walk in my ways, I would feed them with the best of wheat, and with honey from the rock I would fill them." **R**.

Verse before the Gospel: Matthew 4:17

Repent, says the Lord; the Kingdom of heaven is at hand.

Gospel: Mark 12:28-34

One of the scribes came to Jesus and asked him, "Which is the first of all the commandments?" Jesus replied, "The first is this: *Hear, O Israel! The Lord our God is Lord alone! You shall love the Lord your God with all your heart, with all your soul, with all your mind, and with all your strength.* The second is this: *You shall love your neighbor as yourself.* There is no other commandment greater than these." The scribe said to him, "Well said, teacher. You are right in saying, *He is One and there is no other than he.* And *to love him with all your heart, with all your understanding, with all your strength, and to love your neighbor as yourself* is worth more than all burnt offerings and sacrifices." And when Jesus saw that he answered with understanding, he said to him, "You are not far from the Kingdom of God." And no one dared to ask him any more questions.

SATURDAY, MARCH 13

SATURDAY OF THE THIRD WEEK OF LENT

First Reading: Hosea 6:1-6

"Come, let us return to the LORD, it is he who has rent, but he will heal us; he has struck us, but he will bind our wounds. He will revive us after two days; on the third day he will raise us up, to live in his presence. Let us know, let us strive to know the LORD; as certain as the dawn is his coming, and his judgment shines forth like the light of day! He will come to us like the rain, like spring rain that waters the earth." What can I do with you, Ephraim? What can I do with you, Judah? Your piety is like a morning cloud, like the dew that early passes away. For this reason I smote them through the prophets, I slew them by the words of my mouth; for it is love that I desire, not sacrifice, and knowledge of God rather than burnt offerings.

Responsorial Psalm: Psalm 51:3-4, 18-19, 20-21ab
R. (Hosea 6:6) It is mercy I desire, and not sacrifice.

Have mercy on me, O God, in your goodness; in the greatness of your compassion wipe out my offense. Thoroughly wash me from my guilt and of my sin cleanse me. **R.**

For you are not pleased with sacrifices; should I offer a burnt offering, you would not accept it. My sacrifice, O God, is a contrite spirit; a heart contrite and humbled, O God, you will not spurn. **R.**

Be bountiful, O LORD, to Zion in your kindness by rebuilding the walls of Jerusalem; Then shall you be pleased with due sacrifices, burnt offerings and holocausts. **R.**

Verse before the Gospel: Psalm 95:8
If today you hear his voice, harden not your hearts.

Gospel: Luke 18:9-14
Jesus addressed this parable to those who were convinced of their own righteousness and despised everyone else. "Two people went up to the temple area to pray; one was a Pharisee and the other was a tax collector. The Pharisee took up his position and spoke this prayer to himself, 'O God, I thank you that I am not like the rest of humanity —greedy, dishonest, adulterous — or even like this tax collector. I fast twice a week, and I pay tithes on my whole income.' But the tax collector stood off at a distance and would not even raise his eyes to heaven but beat his breast and prayed, 'O God, be merciful to me a sinner.' I tell you, the latter went home justified, not the former; for everyone who exalts himself will be humbled, and the one who humbles himself will be exalted."

First Reading: 1 Samuel 16:1b, 6-7, 10-13a

The LORD said to Samuel: "Fill your horn with oil, and be on your way. I am sending you to Jesse of Bethlehem, for I have chosen my king from among his sons." As Jesse and his sons came to the sacrifice, Samuel looked at Eliab and thought, "Surely the LORD's anointed is here before him." But the LORD said to Samuel: "Do not judge from his appearance or from his lofty stature, because I have rejected him. Not as man sees does God see, because man sees the appearance but the LORD looks into the heart." In the same way Jesse presented seven sons before Samuel, but Samuel said to Jesse, "The LORD has not chosen any one of these." Then Samuel asked Jesse, "Are these all the sons you have?" Jesse replied, "There is still the youngest, who is tending the sheep." Samuel said to Jesse, "Send for him; we will not begin the sacrificial banquet until he arrives here." Jesse sent and had the young man brought to them. He was ruddy, a youth handsome to behold and making a splendid appearance. The LORD said, "There—anoint him, for this is the one!" Then Samuel, with the horn of oil in hand, anointed David in the presence of his brothers; and from that day on, the spirit of the LORD rushed upon David.

Responsorial Psalm: Psalm 23: 1-3a, 3b-4, 5, 6.

R. (1) The Lord is my shepherd; there is nothing I shall want.

The LORD is my shepherd; I shall not want. In verdant pastures he gives me repose; beside restful waters he leads me; he refreshes my soul. **R.**

He guides me in right paths for his name's sake. Even though I walk in the dark valley I fear no evil; for you are at my side with your rod and your staff that give me courage. **R.**

You spread the table before me in the sight of my foes; you anoint my head with oil; my cup overflows. **R.**

Only goodness and kindness follow me all the days of my life; and I shall dwell in the house of the LORD for years to come. **R.**

Second Reading: Ephesians 5:8-14
Brothers and sisters: You were once darkness, but now you are light in the Lord. Live as children of light, for light produces every kind of goodness and righteousness and truth. Try to learn what is pleasing to the Lord. Take no part in the fruitless works of darkness; rather expose them, for it is shameful even to mention the things done by them in secret; but everything exposed by the light becomes visible, for everything that becomes visible is light. Therefore, it says: "Awake, O sleeper, and arise from the dead, and Christ will give you light."

Verse before the Gospel: John 8:12
I am the light of the world, says the Lord; whoever follows me will have the light of life.

Gospel: John 9:1-41 or 9:1, 6-9, 13-17, 34-38
As Jesus passed by he saw a man blind from birth. His disciples asked him, "Rabbi, who sinned, this man or his parents, that he was born blind?" Jesus answered, "Neither he nor his parents sinned; it is so that the works of God might be made visible through him. We have to do the works of the one who sent me while it is day. Night is coming when no one can work. While I am in the world, I am the light of the world." When he had said this, he spat on the ground and made clay with the saliva, and smeared the clay on his eyes, and said to him, "Go wash in the Pool of Siloam" —which means Sent—. So he went and washed, and came back able to see. His neighbors and those who had seen him earlier as a beggar said, "Isn't this the one who used to sit and beg?" Some said, "It is, "but others said, "No, he just looks like him." He said, "I am." So they said to him, "How were your eyes opened?" He replied, "The man called Jesus made clay and anointed my eyes and told me, 'Go to Siloam and wash.' So I went there and washed and was able to see." And they said to him, "Where

is he?" He said, "I don't know." They brought the one who was once blind to the Pharisees. Now Jesus had made clay and opened his eyes on a Sabbath. So then the Pharisees also asked him how he was able to see. He said to them, "He put clay on my eyes, and I washed, and now I can see." So some of the Pharisees said, "This man is not from God, because he does not keep the Sabbath." But others said, "How can a sinful man do such signs?" And there was a division among them. So they said to the blind man again, "What do you have to say about him, since he opened your eyes?" He said, "He is a prophet." Now the Jews did not believe that he had been blind and gained his sight until they summoned the parents of the one who had gained his sight. They asked them, "Is this your son, who you say was born blind? How does he now see?" His parents answered and said, "We know that this is our son and that he was born blind. We do not know how he sees now, nor do we know who opened his eyes. Ask him, he is of age; he can speak for himself." His parents said this because they were afraid of the Jews, for the Jews had already agreed that if anyone acknowledged him as the Christ, he would be expelled from the synagogue. For this reason his parents said, "He is of age; question him." So a second time they called the man who had been blind and said to him, "Give God the praise! We know that this man is a sinner." He replied, "If he is a sinner, I do not know. One thing I do know is that I was blind and now I see." So they said to him, "What did he do to you? How did he open your eyes?" He answered them, "I told you already and you did not listen. Why do you want to hear it again? Do you want to become his disciples, too?" They ridiculed him and said, "You are that man's disciple; we are disciples of Moses! We know that God spoke to Moses, but we do not know where this one is from." The man answered and said to them, "This is what is so amazing, that you do not know where he is from, yet he opened my eyes. We know that God does not listen to sinners, but if one is devout and does his will, he listens to him. It is unheard of that anyone ever opened the eyes of a person born blind. If this man were not from God, he would not be able to do anything." They answered and said to him, "You were born totally in sin, and are you trying to teach us?" Then they threw him out. When Jesus heard that they had thrown him out, he found him and said, do you believe in the Son of Man?" He answered and said, "Who is he, sir, that I may believe in him?" Jesus said to him, "You have seen him, the one speaking with you is he." He said, "I do believe, Lord," and he worshiped him. Then Jesus said, "I came into this world for judgment, so that those who do not see might see, and those who do see might become blind." Some of the Pharisees who were with him heard this and said to him, "Surely we are not also blind, are we?" Jesus said to them, "If you were blind, you would have no sin; but now you are saying, 'We see,' so your sin remains.

Or:
John 9:1, 6-9, 13-17, 34-38
As Jesus passed by he saw a man blind from birth. He spat on the ground and made clay with the saliva, and smeared the clay on his eyes, and said to him, "Go wash in the Pool of Siloam" — which means Sent —. So he went and washed, and came back able to see. His neighbors and those who had seen him earlier as a beggar said, "Isn't this the one who used to sit and beg?" Some said, "It is, "but others said, "No, he just looks like him." He said, "I am." They brought the one who was once blind to the Pharisees. Now Jesus had made clay and opened his eyes on a Sabbath. So then the Pharisees also asked him how he was able to see. He said to them, "He put clay on my eyes, and I washed, and now I can see." So some of the Pharisees said, "This man is not from God, because he does not keep the Sabbath." But others said, "How can a sinful man do such signs?" And there was a division among them. So they said to the blind man again, "What do you have to say about him, since he opened your eyes?" He said, "He is a prophet." They answered and said to him, "You were born totally in sin, and are you trying to teach us?" Then they threw him out. When Jesus heard that they had thrown him out, he found him and said, "Do you believe in the Son

of Man?" He answered and said, "Who is he, sir, that I may believe in him?" Jesus said to him, "You have seen him, and the one speaking with you is he." He said, "I do believe, Lord," and he worshiped him.

First Reading: Isaiah 65:17-21
Thus says the LORD: Lo, I am about to create new heavens and a new earth; the things of the past shall not be remembered or come to mind. Instead, there shall always be rejoicing and happiness in what I create; for I create Jerusalem to be a joy and its people to be a delight; I will rejoice in Jerusalem and exult in my people. No longer shall the sound of weeping be heard there, or the sound of crying; No longer shall there be in it an infant who lives but a few days, or an old man who does not round out his full lifetime; He dies a mere youth who reaches but a hundred years, and he who fails of a hundred shall be thought accursed. They shall live in the houses they build, and eat the fruit of the vineyards they plant.

Responsorial Psalm: Psalm 30:2 and 4, 5-6, 11-12a and 13b
R. (2a) I will praise you, Lord, for you have rescued me.
I will extol you, O LORD, for you drew me clear and did not let my enemies rejoice over me. O LORD, you brought me up from the nether world; you preserved me from among those going down into the pit. **R.**
Sing praise to the LORD, you his faithful ones, and give thanks to his holy name. For his anger lasts but a moment; a lifetime, his good will. At nightfall, weeping enters in, but with the dawn, rejoicing. **R.**
"Hear, O LORD, and have pity on me; O LORD, be my helper." You changed my mourning into dancing; O LORD, my God, forever will I give you thanks. **R.**

Verse before the Gospel: Amos 5:14
Seek good and not evil so that you may live, and the LORD will be

with you.

Gospel: John 4:43-54

At that time Jesus left [Samaria] for Galilee. For Jesus himself testified that a prophet has no honor in his native place. When he came into Galilee, the Galileans welcomed him, since they had seen all he had done in Jerusalem at the feast; for they themselves had gone to the feast. Then he returned to Cana in Galilee, where he had made the water wine. Now there was a royal official whose son was ill in Capernaum. When he heard that Jesus had arrived in Galilee from Judea, he went to him and asked him to come down and heal his son, who was near death. Jesus said to him, "Unless you people see signs and wonders, you will not believe." The royal official said to him, "Sir, come down before my child dies." Jesus said to him, "You may go; your son will live." The man believed what Jesus said to him and left. While the man was on his way back, his slaves met him and told him that his boy would live. He asked them when he began to recover. They told him, "The fever left him yesterday, about one in the afternoon." The father realized that just at that time Jesus had said to him, "Your son will live," and he and his whole household came to believe. Now this was the second sign Jesus did when he came to Galilee from Judea.

TUESDAY, MARCH 16
TUESDAY OF THE FOURTH WEEK OF LENT
First Reading: Ezekiel 47:1-9, 12

The angel brought me, Ezekiel, back to the entrance of the temple of the LORD, and I saw water flowing out from beneath the threshold of the temple toward the east, for the façade of the temple was toward the east; the water flowed down from the right side of the temple, south of the altar. He led me outside by the north gate, and around to the outer gate facing the east, where I saw water trickling from the right side. Then when he had walked off to the east with a measuring cord in his hand, he measured off a thousand cubits and had me wade through the water, which was ankle-deep. He measured off another thousand and once more had me wade through the water, which was now knee-deep. Again he measured off a thousand and had me wade; the water was up to my waist. Once more he measured off a thousand, but there was now a river through which I could not wade; for the water had risen so high it had become a river that could not be crossed except by swimming. He asked me, "Have you seen this, son of man?" Then he brought me to the bank of the river, where he had me sit. Along the bank of the river I saw very many trees on both sides. He said to me, "This water flows into the eastern district down upon the Arabah, and empties into the sea, the salt waters, which it makes fresh. Wherever the river flows, every sort of living creature that can multiply shall live, and there shall be abundant fish, for wherever this water comes the sea shall be made fresh. Along both banks of the river, fruit trees of every kind shall grow; their leaves shall not fade, nor their fruit fail. Every month they shall bear fresh fruit, for they shall be watered by the flow from the sanctuary. Their fruit shall serve for food, and their leaves for medicine."

Responsorial Psalm: Psalm 46:2-3, 5-6, 8-9
R. (8) The Lord of hosts is with us; our stronghold is the God of Jacob.
God is our refuge and our strength, an ever-present help in distress. Therefore we fear not, though the earth be shaken and mountains plunge into the depths of the sea. **R.**
There is a stream whose runlets gladden the city of God, the holy dwelling of the Most High. God is in its midst; it shall not be disturbed; God will help it at the break of dawn. **R.**
The LORD of hosts is with us; our stronghold is the God of Jacob. Come! Behold the deeds of the LORD, the astounding things he has wrought on earth. **R.**

Verse before the Gospel: Psalm 51:12a, 14a

A clean heart create for me, O God; give me back the joy of your salvation.

Gospel: John 5:1-16

There was a feast of the Jews, and Jesus went up to Jerusalem. Now there is in Jerusalem at the Sheep Gate a pool called in Hebrew Bethesda, with five porticoes. In these lay a large number of ill, blind, lame, and crippled. One man was there who had been ill for thirty-eight years. When Jesus saw him lying there and knew that he had been ill for a long time, he said to him, "Do you want to be well?" The sick man answered him, "Sir, I have no one to put me into the pool when the water is stirred up; while I am on my way, someone else gets down there before me." Jesus said to him, "Rise, take up your mat, and walk." Immediately the man became well, took up his mat, and walked. Now that day was a Sabbath. So the Jews said to the man who was cured, "It is the Sabbath, and it is not lawful for you to carry your mat." He answered them, "The man who made me well told me, 'Take up your mat and walk.'" They asked him, "Who is the man who told you, 'Take it up and walk'?" The man who was healed did not know who it was, for Jesus had slipped away, since there was a crowd there. After this Jesus found him in the temple area and said to him, "Look, you are well; do not sin anymore, so that nothing worse may happen to you." The man went and told the Jews that Jesus was the one who had made him well. Therefore, the Jews began to persecute Jesus because he did this on a Sabbath.

WEDNESDAY, MARCH 17
WEDNESDAY OF THE FOURTH WEEK OF LENT

First Reading: Isaiah 49:8-15

Thus says the LORD: In a time of favor I answer you, on the day of salvation I help you; and I have kept you and given you as a covenant to the people, to restore the land and allot the desolate heritages, saying to the prisoners: Come out! To those in darkness: Show yourselves! Along the ways they shall find pasture, on every bare height shall their pastures be. They shall not hunger or thirst, nor shall the scorching wind or the sun strike them; for he who pities them leads them and guides them beside springs of water. I will cut a road through all my mountains, and make my highways level. See, some shall come from afar, others from the north and the west, and some from the land of Syene. Sing out, O heavens, and rejoice, O earth, break forth into song, you mountains. For the LORD comforts his people and shows mercy to his afflicted. But Zion said, "The LORD has forsaken me; my Lord has forgotten me." Can a mother forget her infant, be without tenderness for the child of her womb? Even should she forget, I will never forget you.

Responsorial Psalm: Psalm 145:8-9, 13cd-14, 17-18
R. (8a) The Lord is gracious and merciful.
The LORD is gracious and merciful, slow to anger and of great kindness. The LORD is good to all and compassionate toward all his works. **R.**
The LORD is faithful in all his words and holy in all his works. The LORD lifts up all who are falling and raises up all who are bowed down. **R.**
The LORD is just in all his ways and holy in all his works. The LORD is near to all who call upon him, to all who call upon him in truth. **R.**

Verse before the Gospel: John 11:25a, 26
I am the resurrection and the life, says the Lord; whoever believes in me will never die.

Gospel: John 5:17-30
Jesus answered the Jews: "My Father is at work until now, so I am at work." For this reason they tried all the more to kill him, because he not only broke the Sabbath but he also called God his own father, making himself equal to God. Jesus answered and said to them, "Amen, amen, I say to you, the Son cannot do anything on his own,

but only what he sees the Father doing; for what he does, the Son will do also. For the Father loves the Son and shows him everything that he himself does, and he will show him greater works than these, so that you may be amazed. For just as the Father raises the dead and gives life, so also does the Son give life to whomever he wishes. Nor does the Father judge anyone, but he has given all judgment to the Son, so that all may honor the Son just as they honor the Father. Whoever does not honor the Son does not honor the Father who sent him. Amen, amen, I say to you, whoever hears my word and believes in the one who sent me has eternal life and will not come to condemnation, but has passed from death to life. Amen, amen, I say to you, the hour is coming and is now here when the dead will hear the voice of the Son of God, and those who hear will live. For just as the Father has life in himself, so also he gave to the Son the possession of life in himself. And he gave him power to exercise judgment, because he is the Son of Man. Do not be amazed at this, because the hour is coming in which all who are in the tombs will hear his voice and will come out, those who have done good deeds to the resurrection of life, but those who have done wicked deeds to the resurrection of condemnation. "I cannot do anything on my own; I judge as I hear, and my judgment is just, because I do not seek my own will but the will of the one who sent me."

THURSDAY, MARCH 18
THURSDAY OF THE FOURTH WEEK OF LENT
First Reading: Exodus 32:7-14

The LORD said to Moses, "Go down at once to your people whom you brought out of the land of Egypt, for they have become depraved. They have soon turned aside from the way I pointed out to them, making for themselves a molten calf and worshiping it, sacrificing to it and crying out, 'This is your God, O Israel, who brought you out of the land of Egypt!' The LORD said to Moses, "I see how stiff-necked this people is. Let me alone, then, that my wrath may blaze up against them to consume them. Then I will make of you a great nation." But Moses implored the LORD, his God, saying, "Why, O LORD, should your wrath blaze up against your own people, whom you brought out of the land of Egypt with such great power and with so strong a hand? Why should the Egyptians say, 'With evil intent he brought them out, that he might kill them in the mountains and exterminate them from the face of the earth'? Let your blazing wrath die down; relent in punishing your people. Remember your servants Abraham, Isaac and Israel, and how you swore to them by your own self, saying, 'I will make your descendants as numerous as the stars in the sky; and all this land that I promised, I will give your descendants as their perpetual heritage.'" So the LORD relented in the punishment he had threatened to inflict on his people.

Responsorial Psalm: Psalm 106:19-20, 21-22, 23
R. (4a) Remember us, O Lord, as you favor your people.
Our fathers made a calf in Horeb and adored a molten image; they exchanged their glory for the image of a grass-eating bullock. **R.**
They forgot the God who had saved them, who had done great deeds in Egypt, Wondrous deeds in the land of Ham, terrible things at the Red Sea. **R.**
Then he spoke of exterminating them, but Moses, his chosen one, withstood him in the breach to turn back his destructive wrath. **R.**

Verse before the Gospel: John 3:16
God so loved the world that he gave his only-begotten Son, so that everyone who believes in him might have eternal life.

Gospel: John 5:31-47
Jesus said to the Jews: "If I testify on my own behalf, my testimony is not true. But there is another who testifies on my behalf, and I know that the testimony he gives on my behalf is true. You sent emissaries to John, and he testified to the truth. I do not accept human testimony, but I say this so that you may be saved. He was a burning

and shining lamp, and for a while you were content to rejoice in his light. But I have testimony greater than John's. The works that the Father gave me to accomplish, these works that I perform testify on my behalf that the Father has sent me. Moreover, the Father who sent me has testified on my behalf. But you have never heard his voice nor seen his form, and you do not have his word remaining in you, because you do not believe in the one whom he has sent. You search the Scriptures, because you think you have eternal life through them; even they testify on my behalf. But you do not want to come to me to have life. "I do not accept human praise; moreover, I know that you do not have the love of God in you. I came in the name of my Father, but you do not accept me; yet if another comes in his own name, you will accept him. How can you believe, when you accept praise from one another and do not seek the praise that comes from the only God? Do not think that I will accuse you before the Father: the one who will accuse you is Moses, in whom you have placed your hope. For if you had believed Moses, you would have believed me, because he wrote about me. But if you do not believe his writings, how will you believe my words?"

FRIDAY, MARCH 19
SOLEMNITY OF SAINT JOSEPH, HUSBAND OF THE BLESSED VIRGIN MARY

First Reading: 2 Samuel 7:4-5a, 12-14a, 16

The LORD spoke to Nathan and said: "Go, tell my servant David, 'When your time comes and you rest with your ancestors, I will raise up your heir after you, sprung from your loins, and I will make his kingdom firm. It is he who shall build a house for my name. And I will make his royal throne firm forever. I will be a father to him, and he shall be a son to me. Your house and your kingdom shall endure forever before me; your throne shall stand firm forever.'"

Responsorial Psalm: Psalm 89:2-3, 4-5, 27 and 29
R. (37) The son of David will live for ever.

The promises of the LORD I will sing forever; through all generations my mouth shall proclaim your faithfulness, for you have said, "My kindness is established forever"; in heaven you have confirmed your faithfulness. **R**.

"I have made a covenant with my chosen one, I have sworn to David my servant: Forever will I confirm your posterity and establish your throne for all generations." **R**.

"He shall say of me, 'You are my father, my God, the Rock, my savior.' Forever I will maintain my kindness toward him, and my covenant with him stands firm." **R**.

Second Reading: Romans 4:13, 16-18, 22

Brothers and sisters: It was not through the law that the promise was made to Abraham and his descendants that he would inherit the world, but through the righteousness that comes from faith. For this reason, it depends on faith, so that it may be a gift, and the promise may be guaranteed to all his descendants, not to those who only adhere to the law but to those who follow the faith of Abraham, who is the father of all of us, as it is written, *I have made you father of many nations.* He is our father in the sight of God, in whom he believed, who gives life to the dead and calls into being what does not exist. He believed, hoping against hope, that he would become *the father of many nations,* according to what was said, *thus shall your descendants be.* That is why *it was credited to him as righteousness.*

Verse before the Gospel: Psalm 84:5

Blessed are those who dwell in your house, O Lord; they never cease to praise you.

Gospel: Matthew 1:16, 18-21, 24a or Luke 2:41-51a

Jacob was the father of Joseph, the husband of Mary. Of her was born Jesus who is called the Christ. Now this is how the birth of Jesus Christ came about. When his mother Mary was betrothed to Joseph, but before they lived together, she was found with child through the Holy Spirit. Joseph her husband, since he was a righteous man, yet unwilling to expose her to shame, decided to divorce her quietly. Such was his intention when, behold, the angel of the Lord appeared to him in a dream and said, "Joseph, son of David, do not be afraid to take Mary your wife into your home. For it is through the Holy Spirit that this child has been conceived in her. She will bear a son and you are to name him Jesus, because he will save his people from their sins." When Joseph awoke, he did as the angel of the Lord had commanded him and took his wife into his home.

Or:
Luke 2:41-51a
Each year Jesus' parents went to Jerusalem for the feast of Passover, and when he was twelve years old, they went up according to festival custom. After they had completed its days, as they were returning, the boy Jesus remained behind in Jerusalem, but his parents did not know it. Thinking that he was in the caravan, they journeyed for a day and looked for him among their relatives and acquaintances, but not finding him, they returned to Jerusalem to look for him. After three days they found him in the temple, sitting in the midst of the teachers, listening to them and asking them questions, and all who heard him were astounded at his understanding and his answers. When his parents saw him, they were astonished, and his mother said to him, "Son, why have you done this to us? Your father and I have been looking for you with great anxiety." And he said to them, "Why were you looking for me? Did you not know that I must be in my Father's house?" But they did not understand what he said to them. He went down with them and came to Nazareth, and was obedient to them.

SATURDAY, MARCH 20
SATURDAY OF THE FOURTH WEEK OF LENT
First Reading: Jeremiah 11:18-20
I knew their plot because the LORD informed me; at that time you,

O LORD, showed me their doings. Yet I, like a trusting lamb led to slaughter, had not realized that they were hatching plots against me: "Let us destroy the tree in its vigor; let us cut him off from the land of the living, so that his name will be spoken no more." But, you, O LORD of hosts, O just Judge, searcher of mind and heart, Let me witness the vengeance you take on them, for to you I have entrusted my cause!

Responsorial Psalm: Psalm 7:2-3, 9bc-10, 11-12
R. (2a) O Lord, my God, in you I take refuge.
O LORD, my God, in you I take refuge; save me from all my pursuers and rescue me, lest I become like the lion's prey, to be torn to pieces, with no one to rescue me. **R.**
Do me justice, O LORD, because I am just, and because of the innocence that is mine. Let the malice of the wicked come to an end, but sustain the just, O searcher of heart and soul, O just God. **R.**
A shield before me is God, who saves the upright of heart; a just judge is God, a God who punishes day by day. **R.**

Verse before the Gospel: Luke 8:15
Blessed are they who have kept the word with a generous heart and yield a harvest through perseverance.

Gospel: John 7:40-53
Some in the crowd who heard these words of Jesus said, "This is truly the Prophet." Others said, "This is the Christ." But others said, "The Christ will not come from Galilee, will he? Does not Scripture say that the Christ will be of David's family and come from Bethlehem, the village where David lived?" So a division occurred in the crowd because of him. Some of them even wanted to arrest him, but no one laid hands on him. So the guards went to the chief priests and Pharisees, who asked them, "Why did you not bring him?" The guards answered, "Never before has anyone spoken like this man." So the Pharisees answered them, "Have you also been deceived?

Have any of the authorities or the Pharisees believed in him? But this crowd, which does not know the law, is accursed." Nicodemus, one of their members who had come to him earlier, said to them, "Does our law condemn a man before it first hears him and finds out what he is doing?" They answered and said to him, "You are not from Galilee also, are you? Look and see that no prophet arises from Galilee." Then each went to his own house.

SUNDAY, MARCH 21
FIFTH SUNDAY OF LENT
First Reading: Jeremiah 31:31-34

The days are coming, says the LORD, when I will make a new covenant with the house of Israel and the house of Judah. It will not be like the covenant I made with their fathers the day I took them by the hand to lead them forth from the land of Egypt; for they broke my covenant, and I had to show myself their master, says the LORD. But this is the covenant that I will make with the house of Israel after those days, says the LORD. I will place my law within them and write it upon their hearts; I will be their God, and they shall be my people. No longer will they have need to teach their friends and relatives how to know the LORD. All, from least to greatest, shall know me, says the LORD, for I will forgive their evildoing and remember their sin no more.

Responsorial Psalm: Psalm 51:3-4, 12-13, 14-15
R. (12a) Create a clean heart in me, O God.

Have mercy on me, O God, in your goodness; in the greatness of your compassion wipe out my offense. Thoroughly wash me from my guilt and of my sin cleanse me. **R.**

A clean heart create for me, O God, and a steadfast spirit renew within me. Cast me not out from your presence, and your Holy Spirit take not from me. **R.**

Give me back the joy of your salvation, and a willing spirit sustain in me. I will teach transgressors your ways, and sinners shall return to you. **R**.

Second Reading: Hebrews 5:7-9
In the days when Christ Jesus was in the flesh, he offered prayers and supplications with loud cries and tears to the one who was able to save him from death, and he was heard because of his reverence. Son though he was, he learned obedience from what he suffered; and when he was made perfect, he became the source of eternal salvation for all who obey him.

Verse before the Gospel: John 12:26
Whoever serves me must follow me, says the Lord; and where I am, there also will my servant be.

Gospel: John 12:20-33
Some Greeks who had come to worship at the Passover Feast came to Philip, who was from Bethsaida in Galilee, and asked him, "Sir, we would like to see Jesus." Philip went and told Andrew; then Andrew and Philip went and told Jesus. Jesus answered them, "The hour has come for the Son of Man to be glorified. Amen, amen, I say to you, unless a grain of wheat falls to the ground and dies, it remains just a grain of wheat; but if it dies, it produces much fruit. Whoever loves his life loses it, and whoever hates his life in this world will preserve it for eternal life. Whoever serves me must follow me, and where I am, there also will my servant be. The Father will honor whoever serves me. "I am troubled now. Yet what should I say? 'Father, save me from this hour'? But it was for this purpose that I came to this hour. Father, glorify your name." Then a voice came from heaven, "I have glorified it and will glorify it again." The crowd there heard it and said it was thunder; but others said, "An angel has spoken to him." Jesus answered and said, "This voice did not come for my sake but for yours. Now is the time of judgment on this world; now the ruler of this world will be driven out. And when I am lifted up from the earth, I will draw everyone to myself." He said this indicating the

kind of death he would die.

First Reading: Daniel 13:1-9, 15-17, 19-30, 33-62 or 13:41c-62

In Babylon there lived a man named Joakim, who married a very beautiful and God-fearing woman, Susanna, the daughter of Hilkiah; her pious parents had trained their daughter according to the Law of Moses. Joakim was very rich; he had a garden near his house, and the Jews had recourse to him often because he was the most respected of them all. That year, two elders of the people were appointed judges, of whom the Lord said, "Wickedness has come out of Babylon: from the elders who were to govern the people as judges." These men, to whom all brought their cases, frequented the house of Joakim. When the people left at noon, Susanna used to enter her husband's garden for a walk. When the old men saw her enter every day for her walk, they began to lust for her. They suppressed their consciences; they would not allow their eyes to look to heaven, and did not keep in mind just judgments. One day, while they were waiting for the right moment, she entered the garden as usual, with two maids only. She decided to bathe, for the weather was warm. Nobody else was there except the two elders, who had hidden themselves and were watching her. "Bring me oil and soap," she said to the maids, "and shut the garden doors while I bathe." As soon as the maids had left, the two old men got up and hurried to her. "Look," they said, "the garden doors are shut, and no one can see us; give in to our desire, and lie with us. If you refuse, we will testify against you that you dismissed your maids because a young man was here with you." "I am completely trapped," Susanna groaned. "If I yield, it will be my death; if I refuse, I cannot escape your power. Yet it is better for me to fall into your power without guilt than to sin before the Lord." Then Susanna shrieked, and the old men also shouted at her, as one of them ran to open the garden doors. When the people in the house heard the cries from the garden, they rushed in by the side gate to see what had happened to her. At the accusations by the old men, the servants felt very much ashamed, for never had any such thing been said about Susanna. When the people came to her husband Joakim the next day, the two wicked elders also came, fully determined to put Susanna to death. Before all the people they ordered: "Send for Susanna, the daughter of Hilkiah, the wife of Joakim." When she was sent for, she came with her parents, children and all her relatives. All her relatives and the onlookers were weeping.

In the midst of the people the two elders rose up and laid their hands on her head. Through tears she looked up to heaven, for she trusted in the Lord wholeheartedly. The elders made this accusation: "As we were walking in the garden alone, this woman entered with two girls and shut the doors of the garden, dismissing the girls. A young man, who was hidden there, came and lay with her. When we, in a corner of the garden, saw this crime, we ran toward them. We saw them lying together, but the man we could not hold, because he was stronger than we; he opened the doors and ran off. Then we seized her and asked who the young man was, but she refused to tell us. We testify to this." The assembly believed them, since they were elders and judges of the people, and they condemned her to death. But Susanna cried aloud: "O eternal God, you know what is hidden and are aware of all things before they come to be: you know that they have testified falsely against me. Here I am about to die, though I have done none of the things with which these wicked men have charged me." The Lord heard her prayer. As she was being led to execution, God stirred up the holy spirit of a young boy named Daniel, and he cried aloud: "I will have no part in the death of this woman." All the people turned and asked him, "What is this you are saying?" He stood in their midst and continued, "Are you such fools, O children of Israel! To condemn a woman of Israel without examination and without clear evidence? Return to court, for they have testified falsely against her." Then all the people returned in haste. To Daniel the elders said, "Come, sit with us and inform us, since God has given you the prestige of old age." But he replied,

"Separate these two far from each other that I may examine them."
After they were separated one from the other, he called one of them
and said: "How you have grown evil with age! Now have your past
sins come to term: passing unjust sentences, condemning the
innocent, and freeing the guilty, although the Lord says, 'The
innocent and the just you shall not put to death.' Now, then, if you
were a witness, tell me under what tree you saw them together."
"Under a mastic tree," he answered. Daniel replied, "Your fine lie has
cost you your head, for the angel of God shall receive the sentence
from him and split you in two." Putting him to one side, he ordered
the other one to be brought. Daniel said to him, "Offspring of
Canaan, not of Judah, beauty has seduced you, lust has subverted
your conscience. This is how you acted with the daughters of Israel,
and in their fear they yielded to you; but a daughter of Judah did not
tolerate your wickedness. Now, then, tell me under what tree you
surprised them together." "Under an oak," he said. Daniel replied,
"Your fine lie has cost you also your head, for the angel of God waits
with a sword to cut you in two so as to make an end of you both."
The whole assembly cried aloud, blessing God who saves those who
hope in him. They rose up against the two elders, for by their own
words Daniel had convicted them of perjury. According to the Law
of Moses, they inflicted on them the penalty they had plotted to
impose on their neighbor: they put them to death. Thus was innocent
blood spared that day.

Or:
Daniel 13:41c-62

The assembly condemned Susanna to death. But Susanna cried aloud:
"O eternal God, you know what is hidden and are aware of all things
before they come to be: you know that they have testified falsely
against me. Here I am about to die, though I have done none of the
things with which these wicked men have charged me." The Lord
heard her prayer. As she was being led to execution, God stirred up
the holy spirit of a young boy named Daniel, and he cried aloud: "I

will have no part in the death of this woman." All the people turned and asked him, "What is this you are saying?" He stood in their midst and continued, "Are you such fools, O children of Israel! To condemn a woman of Israel without examination and without clear evidence? Return to court, for they have testified falsely against her." Then all the people returned in haste. To Daniel the elders said, "Come, sit with us and inform us, since God has given you the prestige of old age." But he replied, "Separate these two far from each other that I may examine them." After they were separated one from the other, he called one of them and said: "How you have grown evil with age! Now have your past sins come to term: passing unjust sentences, condemning the innocent, and freeing the guilty, although the Lord says, 'The innocent and the just you shall not put to death.' Now, then, if you were a witness, tell me under what tree you saw them together." "Under a mastic tree," he answered. Daniel replied, "Your fine lie has cost you your head, for the angel of God shall receive the sentence from him and split you in two." Putting him to one side, he ordered the other one to be brought. Daniel said to him, "Offspring of Canaan, not of Judah, beauty has seduced you, lust has subverted your conscience. This is how you acted with the daughters of Israel, and in their fear they yielded to you; but a daughter of Judah did not tolerate your wickedness. Now, then, tell me under what tree you surprised them together." "Under an oak," he said. Daniel replied, "Your fine lie has cost you also your head," for the angel of God waits with a sword to cut you in two so as to make an end of you both." The whole assembly cried aloud, blessing God who saves those who hope in him. They rose up against the two elders, for by their own words Daniel had convicted them of perjury. According to the Law of Moses, they inflicted on them the penalty they had plotted to impose on their neighbor: they put them to death. Thus was innocent blood spared that day.

Responsorial Psalm: Psalm 23:1-3a, 3b-4, 5, 6
R. (4ab) Even though I walk in the dark valley I fear no evil; for

you are at my side.

The LORD is my shepherd; I shall not want. In verdant pastures he gives me repose; beside restful waters he leads me; he refreshes my soul. **R.**

He guides me in right paths for his name's sake. Even though I walk in the dark valley I fear no evil; for you are at my side with your rod and your staff that give me courage. **R**.

You spread the table before me in the sight of my foes; you anoint my head with oil; my cup overflows. **R.**

Only goodness and kindness follow me all the days of my life; and I shall dwell in the house of the LORD for years to come. **R.**

Verse before the Gospel: Ezekiel 33:11

I take no pleasure in the death of the wicked man, says the Lord, but rather in his conversion, that he may live.

Gospel: John 8:1-11

Jesus went to the Mount of Olives. But early in the morning he arrived again in the temple area, and all the people started coming to him, and he sat down and taught them. Then the scribes and the Pharisees brought a woman who had been caught in adultery and made her stand in the middle. They said to him, "Teacher, this woman was caught in the very act of committing adultery. Now in the law, Moses commanded us to stone such women. So what do you say?" They said this to test him, so that they could have some charge to bring against him. Jesus bent down and began to write on the ground with his finger. But when they continued asking him, he straightened up and said to them, "Let the one among you who is without sin be the first to throw a stone at her." Again he bent down and wrote on the ground. And in response, they went away one by one, beginning with the elders. So he was left alone with the woman before him. Then Jesus straightened up and said to her, "Woman, where are they? Has no one condemned you?" She replied, "No one, sir." Then Jesus said, "Neither do I condemn you. Go, and from now on do not sin anymore."

First Reading: Numbers 21:4-9

From Mount Hor the children of Israel set out on the Red Sea road, to bypass the land of Edom. But with their patience worn out by the journey, the people complained against God and Moses, "Why have you brought us up from Egypt to die in this desert, where there is no food or water? We are disgusted with this wretched food!" In punishment the LORD sent among the people saraph serpents, which bit the people so that many of them died. Then the people came to Moses and said, "We have sinned in complaining against the LORD and you. Pray the LORD to take the serpents away from us." So Moses prayed for the people, and the LORD said to Moses, "Make a saraph and mount it on a pole, and whoever looks at it after being bitten will live." Moses accordingly made a bronze serpent and mounted it on a pole, and whenever anyone who had been bitten by a serpent looked at the bronze serpent, he lived.

Responsorial Psalm: Psalm 102:2-3, 16-18, 19-21
R. (2) O Lord, hear my prayer, and let my cry come to you.

O LORD, hear my prayer, and let my cry come to you. Hide not your face from me in the day of my distress. Incline your ear to me; in the day when I call, answer me speedily. **R.**

The nations shall revere your name, O LORD, and all the kings of the earth your glory, When the LORD has rebuilt Zion and appeared in his glory; when he has regarded the prayer of the destitute, and not despised their prayer. **R.**

Let this be written for the generation to come, and let his future creatures praise the LORD: "The LORD looked down from his holy height, from heaven he beheld the earth, to hear the groaning of the prisoners, to release those doomed to die." **R.**

Verse before the Gospel

The seed is the word of God, Christ is the sower; all who come to him will live forever.

Gospel: John 8:21-30

Jesus said to the Pharisees: "I am going away and you will look for me, but you will die in your sin. Where I am going you cannot come." So the Jews said, "He is not going to kill himself, is he, because he said, 'Where I am going you cannot come'?" He said to them, "You belong to what is below, I belong to what is above. You belong to this world, but I do not belong to this world. That is why I told you that you will die in your sins. For if you do not believe that I AM, you will die in your sins." So they said to him, "Who are you?" Jesus said to them, "What I told you from the beginning. I have much to say about you in condemnation. But the one who sent me is true, and what I heard from him I tell the world." They did not realize that he was speaking to them of the Father. So Jesus said to them, "When you lift up the Son of Man, then you will realize that I AM, and that I do nothing on my own, but I say only what the Father taught me. The one who sent me is with me. He has not left me alone, because I always do what is pleasing to him." Because he spoke this way, many came to believe in him.

WEDNESDAY, MARCH 24
WEDNESDAY OF THE FIFTH WEEK OF LENT
First Reading: Daniel 3:14-20, 91-92, 95

King Nebuchadnezzar said: "Is it true, Shadrach, Meshach, and Abednego, that you will not serve my god, or worship the golden statue that I set up? Be ready now to fall down and worship the statue I had made, whenever you hear the sound of the trumpet, flute, lyre, harp, psaltery, bagpipe, and all the other musical instruments; otherwise, you shall be instantly cast into the white-hot furnace; and who is the God who can deliver you out of my hands?" Shadrach, Meshach, and Abednego answered King Nebuchadnezzar,

"There is no need for us to defend ourselves before you in this matter. If our God, whom we serve, can save us from the white-hot furnace and from your hands, O king, may he save us! But even if he will not, know, O king, that we will not serve your god or worship the golden statue that you set up." King Nebuchadnezzar's face became livid with utter rage against Shadrach, Meshach, and Abednego. He ordered the furnace to be heated seven times more than usual and had some of the strongest men in his army bind Shadrach, Meshach, and Abednego and cast them into the white-hot furnace. Nebuchadnezzar rose in haste and asked his nobles, "Did we not cast three men bound into the fire?" "Assuredly, O king," they answered. "But," he replied, "I see four men unfettered and unhurt, walking in the fire, and the fourth looks like a son of God." Nebuchadnezzar exclaimed, "Blessed be the God of Shadrach, Meshach, and Abednego, who sent his angel to deliver the servants who trusted in him; they disobeyed the royal command and yielded their bodies rather than serve or worship any god except their own God."

Responsorial Psalm: Daniel 3:52, 53, 54, 55, 56
R. (52b) Glory and praise forever!
Blessed are you, O Lord, the God of our fathers, praiseworthy and exalted above all forever; and blessed is your holy and glorious name, praiseworthy and exalted above all for all ages. R.
Blessed are you in the temple of your holy glory, praiseworthy and exalted above all forever. **R.**
Blessed are you on the throne of your kingdom, praiseworthy and exalted above all forever. **R.**
Blessed are you who look into the depths from your throne upon the cherubim; praiseworthy and exalted above all forever. **R.**
Blessed are you in the firmament of heaven, praiseworthy and glorious forever. **R.**

Verse before the Gospel: Luke 8:15

Blessed are they who have kept the word with a generous heart and yield a harvest through perseverance.

Gospel: John 8:31-42

Jesus said to those Jews who believed in him, "If you remain in my word, you will truly be my disciples, and you will know the truth, and the truth will set you free." They answered him, "We are descendants of Abraham and have never been enslaved to anyone. How can you say, 'You will become free'?" Jesus answered them, "Amen, amen, I say to you, everyone who commits sin is a slave of sin. A slave does not remain in a household forever, but a son always remains. So if the Son frees you, then you will truly be free. I know that you are descendants of Abraham. But you are trying to kill me, because my word has no room among you. I tell you what I have seen in the Father's presence; then do what you have heard from the Father." They answered and said to him, "Our father is Abraham." Jesus said to them, "If you were Abraham's children, you would be doing the works of Abraham. But now you are trying to kill me, a man who has told you the truth that I heard from God; Abraham did not do this. You are doing the works of your father!" So they said to him, "We were not born of fornication. We have one Father, God." Jesus said to them, "If God were your Father, you would love me, for I came from God and am here; I did not come on my own, but he sent me."

THURSDAY, MARCH 25
SOLEMNITY OF THE ANNUNCIATION OF THE LORD
First Reading: Isaiah 7:10-14; 8:10

The Lord spoke to Ahaz, saying: Ask for a sign from the Lord, your God; let it be deep as the nether world, or high as the sky! But Ahaz answered, "I will not ask! I will not tempt the Lord!" Then Isaiah said: Listen, O house of David! Is it not enough for you to weary people, must you also weary my God? Therefore the Lord himself will give you this sign: the virgin shall be with child, and bear a son, and shall name him Emmanuel, which means "God is with us!"

Responsorial Psalm: Psalm 40:7-8a, 8b-9, 10, 11
R. (8a and 9a) Here I am, Lord; I come to do your will.

Sacrifice or oblation you wished not, but ears open to obedience you gave me. Holocausts or sin-offerings you sought not; then said I, "Behold I come." **R.**

"In the written scroll it is prescribed for me, to do your will, O my God, is my delight, and your law is within my heart!" **R.**

I announced your justice in the vast assembly; I did not restrain my lips, as you, O Lord, know. **R.**

Your justice I kept not hid within my heart; your faithfulness and your salvation I have spoken of; I have made no secret of your kindness and your truth in the vast assembly. **R.**

Second Reading: Hebrews 10:4-10

Brothers and sisters: It is impossible that the blood of bulls and goats take away sins. For this reason, when Christ came into the world, he said: "Sacrifice and offering you did not desire, but a body you prepared for me; in holocausts and sin offerings you took no delight. Then I said, 'As is written of me in the scroll, behold, I come to do your will, O God.'" First he says, "Sacrifices and offerings, holocausts and sin offerings, you neither desired nor delighted in." These are offered according to the law. Then he says, "Behold, I come to do your will." He takes away the first to establish the second. By this "will," we have been consecrated through the offering of the Body of Jesus Christ once for all.

Verse before the Gospel: John 1:14ab
The Word of God became flesh and made his dwelling among us; and we saw his glory.

Gospel: Luke 1:26-38
The angel Gabriel was sent from God to a town of Galilee called Nazareth, to a virgin betrothed to a man named Joseph, of the house

of David, and the virgin's name was Mary. And coming to her, he said, "Hail, full of grace! The Lord is with you." But she was greatly troubled at what was said and pondered what sort of greeting this might be. Then the angel said to her, "Do not be afraid, Mary, for you have found favor with God. Behold, you will conceive in your womb and bear a son, and you shall name him Jesus. He will be great and will be called Son of the Most High, and the Lord God will give him the throne of David his father, and he will rule over the house of Jacob forever, and of his Kingdom there will be no end." But Mary said to the angel, "How can this be, since I have no relations with a man?" And the angel said to her in reply, "The Holy Spirit will come upon you, and the power of the Most High will overshadow you. Therefore the child to be born will be called holy, the Son of God. And behold, Elizabeth, your relative, has also conceived a son in her old age, and this is the sixth month for her who was called barren; for nothing will be impossible for God." Mary said, "Behold, I am the handmaid of the Lord. May it be done to me according to your word." Then the angel departed from her.

FRIDAY, MARCH 26
FRIDAY OF THE FIFTH WEEK OF LENT
First Reading: Jeremiah 20:10-13

I hear the whisperings of many: "Terror on every side! Denounce! Let us denounce him!" All those who were my friends are on the watch for any misstep of mine. "Perhaps he will be trapped; then we can prevail, and take our vengeance on him." But the LORD is with me, like a mighty champion: my persecutors will stumble, they will not triumph. In their failure they will be put to utter shame, to lasting, unforgettable confusion. O LORD of hosts, you who test the just, who probe mind and heart, let me witness the vengeance you take on them, for to you I have entrusted my cause. Sing to the LORD, praise the LORD, for he has rescued the life of the poor from the power of the wicked!

Responsorial Psalm: Psalm 18:2-3a, 3bc-4, 5-6, 7

R. (7) In my distress I called upon the Lord, and he heard my voice.

I love you, O LORD, my strength, O LORD, my rock, my fortress, my deliverer. **R.**

My God, my rock of refuge, my shield, the horn of my salvation, my stronghold!

Praised be the LORD, I exclaim, and I am safe from my enemies. **R.**

The breakers of death surged round about me, the destroying floods overwhelmed me; the cords of the nether world enmeshed me, the snares of death overtook me. **R.**

In my distress I called upon the LORD and cried out to my God; from his temple he heard my voice, and my cry to him reached his ears. **R.**

Verse before the Gospel: John 6:63c, 68c

Your words, Lord, are Spirit and life; you have the words of everlasting life.

Gospel: John 10:31-42

The Jews picked up rocks to stone Jesus. Jesus answered them, "I have shown you many good works from my Father. For which of these are you trying to stone me?" The Jews answered him, "We are not stoning you for a good work but for blasphemy. You, a man, are making yourself God." Jesus answered them, "Is it not written in your law, 'I said, 'You are gods'"? If it calls them gods to whom the word of God came, and Scripture cannot be set aside, can you say that the one whom the Father has consecrated and sent into the world blasphemes because I said, 'I am the Son of God'? If I do not perform my Father's works, do not believe me; but if I perform them, even if you do not believe me, believe the works, so that you may realize and understand that the Father is in me and I am in the Father." Then they tried again to arrest him; but he escaped from their power. He went back across the Jordan to the place where John first baptized, and there he remained. Many came to him and said, "John performed no sign, but everything John said about this man was true." And many there began to believe in him.

First Reading: Ezekiel 37:21-28

Thus says the Lord GOD: I will take the children of Israel from among the nations to which they have come, and gather them from all sides to bring them back to their land. I will make them one nation upon the land, in the mountains of Israel, and there shall be one prince for them all. Never again shall they be two nations, and never again shall they be divided into two kingdoms. No longer shall they defile themselves with their idols, their abominations, and all their transgressions. I will deliver them from all their sins of apostasy, and cleanse them so that they may be my people and I may be their God. My servant David shall be prince over them, and there shall be one shepherd for them all; they shall live by my statutes and carefully observe my decrees. They shall live on the land that I gave to my servant Jacob, the land where their fathers lived; they shall live on it forever, they, and their children, and their children's children, with my servant David their prince forever. I will make with them a covenant of peace; it shall be an everlasting covenant with them, and I will multiply them, and put my sanctuary among them forever. My dwelling shall be with them; I will be their God, and they shall be my people. Thus the nations shall know that it is I, the LORD, who make Israel holy, when my sanctuary shall be set up among them forever.

Responsorial Psalm: Jeremiah 31:10, 11-12abcd, 13
R. (10d) The Lord will guard us, as a shepherd guards his flock.
Hear the word of the LORD, O nations, proclaim it on distant isles, and say: He who scattered Israel, now gathers them together, he guards them as a shepherd his flock. **R.**

The LORD shall ransom Jacob, he shall redeem him from the hand of his conqueror. Shouting, they shall mount the heights of Zion, they shall come streaming to the LORD's blessings: The grain, the wine, and the oil, the sheep and the oxen. **R**.

Then the virgins shall make merry and dance, and young men and old as well. I will turn their mourning into joy, I will console and gladden them after their sorrows. **R**.

Verse before the Gospel: Ezekiel 18:31

Cast away from you all the crimes you have committed, says the LORD, and make for yourselves a new heart and a new spirit.

Gospel: John 11:45-56

Many of the Jews who had come to Mary and seen what Jesus had done began to believe in him. But some of them went to the Pharisees and told them what Jesus had done. So the chief priests and the Pharisees convened the Sanhedrin and said, "What are we going to do? This man is performing many signs. If we leave him alone, all will believe in him, and the Romans will come and take away both our land and our nation." But one of them, Caiaphas, who was high priest that year, said to them, "You know nothing, nor do you consider that it is better for you that one man should die instead of the people, so that the whole nation may not perish." He did not say this on his own, but since he was high priest for that year, he prophesied that Jesus was going to die for the nation, and not only for the nation, but also to gather into one the dispersed children of God. So from that day on they planned to kill him. So Jesus no longer walked about in public among the Jews, but he left for the region near the desert, to a town called Ephraim, and there he remained with his disciples. Now the Passover of the Jews was near, and many went up from the country to Jerusalem before Passover to purify themselves. They looked for Jesus and said to one another as they were in the temple area, "What do you think? That he will not come to the feast?"

PALM SUNDAY OF THE LORD'S PASSION
AT THE PROCESSION WITH PALMS
Gospel: Mark 11:1-10 or John 12:12-16

When Jesus and his disciples drew near to Jerusalem, to Bethphage and Bethany at the Mount of Olives, he sent two of his disciples and said to them, "Go into the village opposite you, and immediately on entering it, you will find a colt tethered on which no one has ever sat. Untie it and bring it here. If anyone should say to you, 'Why are you doing this?' reply, 'The Master has need of it and will send it back here at once.'" So they went off and found a colt tethered at a gate outside on the street, and they untied it. Some of the bystanders said to them, "What are you doing, untying the colt?" They answered them just as Jesus had told them to, and they permitted them to do it. So they brought the colt to Jesus and put their cloaks over it. And he sat on it. Many people spread their cloaks on the road, and others spread leafy branches that they had cut from the fields. Those preceding him as well as those following kept crying out: "Hosanna! Blessed is he who comes in the name of the Lord! Blessed is the kingdom of our father David that is to come! Hosanna in the highest!"

Or:

John 12:12-16

When the great crowd that had come to the feast heard that Jesus was coming to Jerusalem, they took palm branches and went out to meet him, and cried out: "Hosanna! "Blessed is he who comes in the name of the Lord, the king of Israel." Jesus found an ass and sat upon it, as is written: Fear no more, O daughter Zion; see, your king comes, seated upon an ass's colt. His disciples did not understand this at first, but when Jesus had been glorified they remembered that these things were written about him and that they had done this for him.

First Reading: Isaiah 50:4-7

The Lord GOD has given me a well-trained tongue, that I might know how to speak to the weary a word that will rouse them. Morning after morning he opens my ear that I may hear; and I have not rebelled, have not turned back. I gave my back to those who beat me, my cheeks to those who plucked my beard; my face I did not shield from buffets and spitting. The Lord GOD is my help, therefore I am not disgraced; I have set my face like flint, knowing that I shall not be put to shame.

Responsorial Psalm: Psalm 22:8-9, 17-18, 19-20, 23-24
R. (2a) My God, my God, why have you abandoned me?

All who see me scoff at me; they mock me with parted lips, they wag their heads: "He relied on the LORD; let him deliver him, let him rescue him, if he loves him." **R.**

Indeed, many dogs surround me, a pack of evildoers closes in upon me; they have pierced my hands and my feet; I can count all my bones. **R.**

They divide my garments among them, and for my vesture they cast lots. But you, O LORD, be not far from me; O my help, hasten to aid me. **R.**

I will proclaim your name to my brethren; in the midst of the assembly I will praise you: "You who fear the LORD, praise him; all you descendants of Jacob, give glory to him; revere him, all you descendants of Israel!" **R.**

Second Reading: Philippians 2:6-11

Christ Jesus, though he was in the form of God, did not regard equality with God something to be grasped. Rather, he emptied himself, taking the form of a slave, coming in human likeness; and found human in appearance, he humbled himself, becoming obedient to the point of death, even death on a cross. Because of this, God greatly exalted him and bestowed on him the name which is above every name, that at the name of Jesus every knee should bend, of those in heaven and on earth and under the earth, and every tongue confess that Jesus Christ is Lord, to the glory of God the Father.

Verse before the Gospel: Philippians 2:8-9
Christ became obedient to the point of death, even death on a cross. Because of this, God greatly exalted him and bestowed on him the name which is above every name.

Gospel: Mark 14:1-15:47 or Mark 15:1-39
The Passover and the Feast of Unleavened Bread were to take place in two days' time. So the chief priests and the scribes were seeking a way to arrest him by treachery and put him to death. They said, "Not during the festival, for fear that there may be a riot among the people." When he was in Bethany reclining at table in the house of Simon the leper, a woman came with an alabaster jar of perfumed oil, costly genuine spikenard. She broke the alabaster jar and poured it on his head. There were some who were indignant. "Why has there been this waste of perfumed oil? It could have been sold for more than three hundred days' wages and the money given to the poor." They were infuriated with her. Jesus said, "Let her alone. Why do you make trouble for her? She has done a good thing for me. The poor you will always have with you, and whenever you wish you can do good to them, but you will not always have me. She has done what she could. She has anticipated anointing my body for burial. Amen, I say to you, wherever the gospel is proclaimed to the whole world, what she has done will be told in memory of her." Then Judas Iscariot, one of the Twelve, went off to the chief priests to hand him over to them. When they heard him they were pleased and promised to pay him money. Then he looked for an opportunity to hand him over.

On the first day of the Feast of Unleavened Bread, when they sacrificed the Passover lamb, his disciples said to him, "Where do you want us to go and prepare for you to eat the Passover?" He sent two of his disciples and said to them, "Go into the city and a man will meet you, carrying a jar of water. Follow him. Wherever he enters, say to the master of the house, 'The Teacher says, "Where is my guest room where I may eat the Passover with my disciples?"' Then he will show you a large upper room furnished and ready. Make the preparations for us there." The disciples then went off, entered the city, and found it just as he had told them; and they prepared the Passover. When it was evening, he came with the Twelve. And as they reclined at table and were eating, Jesus said, "Amen, I say to you, one of you will betray me, one who is eating with me." They began to be distressed and to say to him, one by one, "Surely it is not I?" He said to them, "One of the Twelve, the one who dips with me into the dish. For the Son of Man indeed goes, as it is written of him, but woe to that man by whom the Son of Man is betrayed. It would be better for that man if he had never been born." While they were eating, he took bread, said the blessing, broke it, and gave it to them, and said, "Take it; this is my body." Then he took a cup, gave thanks, and gave it to them, and they all drank from it. He said to them, "This is my blood of the covenant, which will be shed for many. Amen, I say to you, I shall not drink again the fruit of the vine until the day when I drink it new in the kingdom of God." Then, after singing a hymn, they went out to the Mount of Olives. Then Jesus said to them, "All of you will have your faith shaken, for it is written: *I will strike the shepherd, and the sheep will be dispersed.* But after I have been raised up, I shall go before you to Galilee." Peter said to him, "Even though all should have their faith shaken, mine will not be." Then Jesus said to him, "Amen, I say to you, this very night before the cock crows twice you will deny me three times. But he vehemently replied, "Even though I should have to die with you, I will not deny you." And they all spoke similarly. Then they came to a place named Gethsemane, and he said to his disciples, "Sit here while I pray." He took with him Peter, James, and John, and began to be troubled and distressed. Then he said to them, "My soul is sorrowful even to death. Remain here and keep watch." He advanced a little and fell to the ground and prayed that if it were possible the hour might pass by him; he said, "Abba, Father, all things are possible to you. Take this cup away from me, but not what I will but what you will." When he returned he found them asleep. He said to Peter, "Simon, are you asleep? Could you not keep watch for one hour? Watch and pray that you may not undergo the test. The spirit is willing but the flesh is weak." Withdrawing again, he prayed, saying the same thing. Then he returned once more and found them asleep, for they could not keep their eyes open and did not know what to answer him. He returned a third time and said to them, "Are you still sleeping and taking your rest? It is enough. The hour has come. Behold, the Son of Man is to be handed over to sinners. Get up, let us go. See, my betrayer is at hand." Then, while he was still speaking, Judas, one of the Twelve, arrived, accompanied by a crowd with swords and clubs who had come from the chief priests, the scribes, and the elders. His betrayer had arranged a signal with them, saying, "The man I shall kiss is the one; arrest him and lead him away securely." He came and immediately went over to him and said, "Rabbi." And he kissed him. At this they laid hands on him and arrested him. One of the bystanders drew his sword, struck the high priest's servant, and cut off his ear. Jesus said to them in reply, "Have you come out as against a robber, with swords and clubs, to seize me? Day after day I was with you teaching in the temple area, yet you did not arrest me; but that the Scriptures may be fulfilled." And they all left him and fled. Now a young man followed him wearing nothing but a linen cloth about his body. They seized him, but he left the cloth behind and ran off naked. They led Jesus away to the high priest, and all the chief priests and the elders and the scribes came together. Peter followed him at a distance into the high priest's courtyard and was seated with the guards, warming himself at the fire. The chief priests and the entire Sanhedrin kept trying to obtain testimony against Jesus in order to put him to death, but they found none. Many gave false witness against him, but their testimony did not agree. Some took the stand and testified falsely against him, alleging, "We heard him say, 'I will destroy this temple made with hands and within three days I will build another not made with hands.'" Even so their testimony did not agree. The high priest rose before the assembly and questioned Jesus, saying, "Have you no answer? What are these men testifying against you?" But he was silent and answered nothing. Again the high priest asked him and said to him, "Are you the Christ, the son of the Blessed One?" Then Jesus answered, "I am; and 'you will see the Son of Man seated at the right hand of the Power and coming with the clouds of heaven.'" At that the high priest tore his garments and said, "What further need have we of witnesses? You have heard the blasphemy. What do you think?" They all condemned him as deserving to die. Some began to spit on him. They blindfolded him and struck him and said to him, "Prophesy!" And the guards greeted him with blows. While Peter was below in the courtyard, one of the high priest's maids came along. Seeing Peter warming himself, she looked intently at him and said, "You too were with the Nazarene, Jesus." But he denied it saying, "I neither know nor understand what you are talking about." So he went out into the outer court. Then the cock crowed. The maid saw him and began again to say to the bystanders, "This man is one of them." Once again he denied it. A little later the bystanders said to Peter once more, "Surely you are one of them; for you too are a Galilean." He began to curse and to swear, "I do not know this man about whom you are talking." And immediately a cock crowed a second time. Then Peter remembered the word that Jesus had said to him, "Before the cock crows twice you will deny me three times." He broke down and wept.

As soon as morning came, the chief priests with the elders and the scribes, that is, the whole Sanhedrin held a council. They bound Jesus, led him away, and handed him over to Pilate. Pilate questioned him, "Are you the king of the Jews?" He said to him in reply, "You say so." The chief priests accused him of many things. Again Pilate questioned him, "Have you no answer? See how many things they accuse you of." Jesus gave him no further answer, so that Pilate was amazed. Now on the occasion of the feast he used to release to them one prisoner whom they requested. A man called Barabbas was then in prison along with the rebels who had committed murder in a rebellion. The crowd came forward and began to ask him to do for them as he was accustomed. Pilate answered, "Do you want me to release to you the king of the Jews?" For he knew that it was out of envy that the chief priests had handed him over. But the chief priests stirred up the crowd to have him release Barabbas for them instead. Pilate again said to them in reply, "Then what do you want me to do with the man you call the king of the Jews?" They shouted again, "Crucify him." Pilate said to them, "Why? What evil has he done?" They only shouted the louder, "Crucify him." So Pilate, wishing to satisfy the crowd, released Barabbas to them and, after he had Jesus scourged, handed him over to be crucified. The soldiers led him away inside the palace, that is, the praetorium, and assembled the whole cohort. They clothed him in purple and, weaving a crown of thorns, placed it on him. They began to salute him with, "Hail, King of the Jews!" and kept striking his head with a reed and spitting upon him. They knelt before him in homage. And when they had mocked him, they stripped him of the purple cloak, dressed him in his own clothes, and led him out to crucify him. They pressed into service a passer-by, Simon, a Cyrenian, who was coming in from the country, the father of Alexander and Rufus, to carry his cross. they brought him to the place of Golgotha— which is translated Place of the Skull —, They gave him wine drugged with myrrh, but he did not take it. Then they crucified him and divided his garments by casting lots for them to see what each should take. It was nine o'clock in the morning when they crucified him. The inscription of the charge against him read, "The King of the Jews." With him they crucified two revolutionaries, one on his right and one on his left. Those passing by reviled him shaking their heads and saying, "Aha! You who would destroy the temple and rebuild it in three days, save yourself by coming down from the cross." Likewise the chief priests, with the scribes, mocked him among themselves and said, "He saved others; he cannot save himself. Let the Christ, the King of Israel, come down now from the cross that we may see and believe." Those who were crucified with him also kept abusing him. At noon darkness came over the whole land until three in the afternoon. And at three o'clock Jesus cried out in a loud voice, "*Eloi, Eloi, lema sabachthani?*" which is translated, "My God, my God, why have you forsaken me?" Some of the bystanders who heard it said, "Look, he is calling Elijah." One of them ran, soaked a sponge with wine, put it on a reed and gave it to him to drink saying, "Wait, let us see if Elijah comes to take him down." Jesus gave a loud cry and breathed his last. The veil of the sanctuary was torn in two from top to bottom. When the centurion who stood facing him saw how he breathed his last he said, "Truly this man was the Son of God!" There were also women looking on from a distance. Among them were Mary Magdalene, Mary the mother of the younger James and of Joses, and Salome. These women had followed him when he was in Galilee and ministered to him. There were also many other women who had come up with him to Jerusalem.

When it was already evening, since it was the day of preparation, the day before the sabbath, Joseph of Arimathea, a distinguished member of the council, who was himself awaiting the kingdom of God, came and courageously went to Pilate and asked for the body of Jesus. Pilate was amazed that he was already dead. He summoned the centurion and asked him if Jesus had already died. And when he learned of it from the centurion, he gave the body to Joseph. Having bought a linen cloth, he took him down, wrapped him in the linen cloth, and laid him in a tomb that had been hewn out of the rock. Then he rolled a stone against the entrance to the tomb. Mary Magdalene and Mary the mother of Joses watched where he was laid.

Or:
Mark 15:1-39
As soon as morning came, the chief priests with the elders and the scribes, that is, the whole Sanhedrin held a council. They bound Jesus, led him away, and handed him over to Pilate. Pilate questioned

him, "Are you the king of the Jews?" He said to him in reply, "You say so." The chief priests accused him of many things. Again Pilate questioned him, "Have you no answer? See how many things they accuse you of." Jesus gave him no further answer, so that Pilate was amazed. Now on the occasion of the feast he used to release to them one prisoner whom they requested. A man called Barabbas was then in prison along with the rebels who had committed murder in a rebellion. The crowd came forward and began to ask him to do for them as he was accustomed. Pilate answered, "Do you want me to release to you the king of the Jews?" For he knew that it was out of envy that the chief priests had handed him over. But the chief priests stirred up the crowd to have him release Barabbas for them instead. Pilate again said to them in reply, "Then what do you want me to do with the man you call the king of the Jews?" They shouted again, "Crucify him." Pilate said to them, "Why? What evil has he done?" They only shouted the louder, "Crucify him." So Pilate, wishing to satisfy the crowd, released Barabbas to them and, after he had Jesus scourged, handed him over to be crucified. The soldiers led him away inside the palace, that is, the praetorium, and assembled the whole cohort. They clothed him in purple and, weaving a crown of thorns, placed it on him. They began to salute him with, "Hail, King of the Jews!" and kept striking his head with a reed and spitting upon him. They knelt before him in homage. And when they had mocked him, they stripped him of the purple cloak, dressed him in his own clothes, and led him out to crucify him. They pressed into service a passer-by, Simon, a Cyrenian, who was coming in from the country, the father of Alexander and Rufus, to carry his cross. They brought him to the place of Golgotha—which is translated Place of the Skull— they gave him wine drugged with myrrh, but he did not take it. Then they crucified him and divided his garments by casting lots for them to see what each should take. It was nine o'clock in the morning when they crucified him. The inscription of the charge against him read, "The King of the Jews." With him they crucified two revolutionaries, one on his right and one on his left. Those passing by reviled him, shaking their heads and saying, "Aha! You who would destroy the temple and rebuild it in three days, save yourself by coming down from the cross." Likewise the chief priests, with the scribes, mocked him among themselves and said, "He saved others; he cannot save himself. Let the Christ, the King of Israel, come down now from the cross that we may see and believe." Those who were crucified with him also kept abusing him. At noon darkness came over the whole land until three in the afternoon. And at three o'clock Jesus cried out in a loud voice, "*Eloi, Eloi, lema sabachthani?*" which is translated, "My God, my God, why have you forsaken me?" Some of the bystanders who heard it said, "Look, he is calling Elijah." One of them ran, soaked a sponge with wine, put it on a reed and gave it to him to drink saying, "Wait, let us see if Elijah comes to take him down." Jesus gave a loud cry and breathed his last. The veil of the sanctuary was torn in two from top to bottom. When the centurion who stood facing him saw how he breathed his last he said, "Truly this man was the Son of God!"

MONDAY, MARCH 29
MONDAY OF HOLY WEEK
First Reading: Isaiah 42:1-7
Here is my servant whom I uphold, my chosen one with whom I am pleased, upon whom I have put my Spirit; he shall bring forth justice to the nations, not crying out, not shouting, not making his voice heard in the street. A bruised reed he shall not break, and a smoldering wick he shall not quench, until he establishes justice on the earth; the coastlands will wait for his teaching. Thus says God, the LORD, who created the heavens and stretched them out, who spreads out the earth with its crops, Who gives breath to its people and spirit to those who walk on it: I, the LORD, have called you for the victory of justice, I have grasped you by the hand; I formed you, and set you as a covenant of the people, a light for the nations, To open the eyes of the blind, to bring out prisoners from confinement, and from the dungeon, those who live in darkness.

Responsorial Psalm: Psalm 27:1, 2, 3, 13-14
R. (1a) The Lord is my light and my salvation.
The LORD is my light and my salvation; whom should I fear? The LORD is my life's refuge; of whom should I be afraid? **R.**
When evildoers come at me to devour my flesh, my foes and my enemies themselves stumble and fall. **R.**
Though an army encamp against me, my heart will not fear; though war be waged upon me, even then will I trust. **R.**
I believe that I shall see the bounty of the LORD in the land of the living. Wait for the LORD with courage; be stouthearted, and wait for the LORD. **R.**

Verse before the Gospel
Hail to you, our King; you alone are compassionate with our faults.

Gospel: John 12:1-11
Six days before Passover Jesus came to Bethany, where Lazarus was, whom Jesus had raised from the dead. They gave a dinner for him there, and Martha served, while Lazarus was one of those reclining at table with him. Mary took a liter of costly perfumed oil made from genuine aromatic nard and anointed the feet of Jesus and dried them with her hair; the house was filled with the fragrance of the oil. Then Judas the Iscariot, one of his disciples, and the one who would betray him, said, "Why was this oil not sold for three hundred days' wages and given to the poor?" He said this not because he cared about the poor but because he was a thief and held the money bag and used to steal the contributions. So Jesus said, "Leave her alone. Let her keep this for the day of my burial. You always have the poor with you, but you do not always have me." The large crowd of the Jews found out that he was there and came, not only because of him, but also to see Lazarus, whom he had raised from the dead. And the chief priests plotted to kill Lazarus too, because many of the Jews were turning away and believing in Jesus because of him.

First Reading: Isaiah 49:1-6

Hear me, O islands, listen, O distant peoples. The LORD called me from birth, from my mother's womb he gave me my name. He made of me a sharp-edged sword and concealed me in the shadow of his arm. He made me a polished arrow, in his quiver he hid me. You are my servant, he said to me, Israel, through whom I show my glory. Though I thought I had toiled in vain, and for nothing, uselessly, spent my strength, yet my reward is with the LORD, my recompense is with my God. For now the LORD has spoken who formed me as his servant from the womb, That Jacob may be brought back to him and Israel gathered to him; and I am made glorious in the sight of the LORD, and my God is now my strength! It is too little, he says, for you to be my servant, to raise up the tribes of Jacob, and restore the survivors of Israel; I will make you a light to the nations, that my salvation may reach to the ends of the earth.

Responsorial Psalm: Psalm 71:1-2, 3-4a, 5ab-6ab, 15 and 17
R. (15ab) I will sing of your salvation.

In you, O LORD, I take refuge; let me never be put to shame. In your justice rescue me, and deliver me; incline your ear to me, and save me. **R.**

Be my rock of refuge, a stronghold to give me safety, for you are my rock and my fortress. O my God, rescue me from the hand of the wicked. **R.**

For you are my hope, O LORD; my trust, O God, from my youth. On you I depend from birth; from my mother's womb you are my strength. **R.**

My mouth shall declare your justice, day by day your salvation. O God, you have taught me from my youth, and till the present I proclaim your wondrous deeds. **R.**

Verse before the Gospel

Hail to you, our King, obedient to the Father; you were led to your crucifixion like a gentle lamb to the slaughter.

Gospel: John 13:21-33, 36-38

Reclining at table with his disciples, Jesus was deeply troubled and testified, "Amen, amen, I say to you, one of you will betray me." The disciples looked at one another, at a loss as to whom he meant. One of his disciples, the one whom Jesus loved, was reclining at Jesus' side. So Simon Peter nodded to him to find out whom he meant. He leaned back against Jesus' chest and said to him, "Master, who is it?" Jesus answered, "It is the one to whom I hand the morsel after I have dipped it." So he dipped the morsel and took it and handed it to Judas, son of Simon the Iscariot. After Judas took the morsel, Satan entered him. So Jesus said to him, "What you are going to do, do quickly." Now none of those reclining at table realized why he said this to him. Some thought that since Judas kept the money bag, Jesus had told him, "Buy what we need for the feast," or to give something to the poor. So Judas took the morsel and left at once. And it was night. When he had left, Jesus said, "Now is the Son of Man glorified, and God is glorified in him. If God is glorified in him, God will also glorify him in himself, and he will glorify him at once. My children, I will be with you only a little while longer. You will look for me, and as I told the Jews, 'Where I go you cannot come,' so now I say it to you." Simon Peter said to him, "Master, where are you going?" Jesus answered him, "Where I am going, you cannot follow me now, though you will follow later." Peter said to him, "Master, why can I not follow you now? I will lay down my life for you." Jesus answered, "Will you lay down your life for me? Amen, amen, I say to you, the cock will not crow before you deny me three times."

WEDNESDAY, MARCH 31
WEDNESDAY OF HOLY WEEK
First Reading: Isaiah 50:4-9a

The Lord GOD has given me a well-trained tongue, that I might know how to speak to the weary a word that will rouse them. Morning after morning he opens my ear that I may hear; And I have not rebelled, have not turned back. I gave my back to those who beat me, my cheeks to those who plucked my beard; my face I did not shield from buffets and spitting. The Lord GOD is my help, therefore I am not disgraced; I have set my face like flint, knowing that I shall not be put to shame. He is near who upholds my right; if anyone wishes to oppose me, let us appear together. Who disputes my right? Let him confront me. See, the Lord GOD is my help; who will prove me wrong?

Responsorial Psalm: Psalm 69:8-10, 21-22, 31 and 33-34
R. (14c) Lord, in your great love, answer me.

For your sake I bear insult, and shame covers my face. I have become an outcast to my brothers, a stranger to my mother's sons, because zeal for your house consumes me, and the insults of those who blaspheme you fall upon me. **R.**

Insult has broken my heart, and I am weak, I looked for sympathy, but there was none; for consolers, not one could I find. Rather they put gall in my food, and in my thirst they gave me vinegar to drink. **R**.

I will praise the name of God in song, and I will glorify him with thanksgiving: "See, you lowly ones, and be glad; you who seek God, may your hearts revive! For the LORD hears the poor, and his own who are in bonds he spurns not." **R.**

Verse before the Gospel
Hail to you, our King; you alone are compassionate with our errors.
Or:
Hail to you, our King, obedient to the Father; you were led to your crucifixion like a gentle lamb to the slaughter.

Gospel: Matthew 26:14-25

One of the Twelve, who was called Judas Iscariot, went to the chief priests and said, "What are you willing to give me if I hand him over to you?" They paid him thirty pieces of silver, and from that time on he looked for an opportunity to hand him over. On the first day of the Feast of Unleavened Bread, the disciples approached Jesus and said, "Where do you want us to prepare for you to eat the Passover?" He said, "Go into the city to a certain man and tell him, 'The teacher says, my appointed time draws near; in your house I shall celebrate the Passover with my disciples.'" The disciples then did as Jesus had ordered, and prepared the Passover.

When it was evening, he reclined at table with the Twelve. And while they were eating, he said, "Amen, I say to you, one of you will betray me." Deeply distressed at this, they began to say to him one after another, "Surely it is not I, Lord?" He said in reply, "He who has dipped his hand into the dish with me is the one who will betray me. The Son of Man indeed goes, as it is written of him, but woe to that man by whom the Son of Man is betrayed. It would be better for that man if he had never been born." Then Judas, his betrayer, said in reply, "Surely it is not I, Rabbi?" He answered, "You have said so."

THURSDAY, APRIL 1
HOLY THURSDAY
(Chrism Mass and Evening Mass of the Lord's Supper)

HOLY THURSDAY: CHRISM MASS
First Reading: Isaiah 61:1-3a, 6a, 8b-9

The Spirit of the Lord GOD is upon me, because the LORD has anointed me; He has sent me to bring glad tidings to the lowly, to heal the brokenhearted, to proclaim liberty to the captives and release to the prisoners, to announce a year of favor from the LORD and a day of vindication by our God, to comfort all who mourn; To place on those who mourn in Zion a diadem instead of ashes, To give them oil of gladness in place of mourning, a glorious mantle instead of a listless spirit. You yourselves shall be named priests of the

LORD, ministers of our God shall you be called. I will give them their recompense faithfully, a lasting covenant I will make with them. Their descendants shall be renowned among the nations, and their offspring among the peoples; all who see them shall acknowledge them as a race the LORD has blessed.

Responsorial Psalm: Psalm 89:21-22, 25 and 27
R. (2) For ever I will sing the goodness of the Lord.

"I have found David, my servant; with my holy oil I have anointed him. That my hand may always be with him; and that my arm may make him strong." **R.**

"My faithfulness and my mercy shall be with him; and through my name shall his horn be exalted. He shall say of me, 'You are my father, my God, the Rock, my savior!'" **R.**

Second Reading: Revelation 1:5-8

[Grace to you and peace] from Jesus Christ, who is the faithful witness, the firstborn of the dead and ruler of the kings of the earth. To him who loves us and has freed us from our sins by his Blood, who has made us into a Kingdom, priests for his God and Father, to him be glory and power forever and ever. Amen. Behold, he is coming amid the clouds, and every eye will see him, even those who pierced him. All the peoples of the earth will lament him. Yes. Amen. "I am the Alpha and the Omega," says the Lord God, "the one who is and who was and who is to come, the Almighty."

Verse before the Gospel: Isaiah 61:1 (cited in Luke 4:18)

The Spirit of the LORD is upon me; for he has sent me to bring glad tidings to the poor.

Gospel: Luke 4:16-21

Jesus came to Nazareth, where he had grown up, and went according to his custom into the synagogue on the Sabbath day. He stood up to read and was handed a scroll of the prophet Isaiah. He unrolled the scroll and found the passage where it was written: *The Spirit of the Lord is upon me, because he has anointed me to bring glad tidings to the poor. He has sent me to proclaim liberty to captives and recovery of sight to the blind, to let the oppressed go free, and to proclaim a year acceptable to the Lord.* Rolling up the scroll, he handed it back to the attendant and sat down, and the eyes of all in the synagogue looked intently at him. He said to them, "Today this Scripture passage is fulfilled in your hearing."

HOLY THURSDAY: EVENING MASS OF THE LORD'S SUPPER

First Reading: Exodus 12:1-8, 11-14

The LORD said to Moses and Aaron in the land of Egypt, "This month shall stand at the head of your calendar; you shall reckon it the first month of the year. Tell the whole community of Israel: On the tenth of this month every one of your families must procure for itself a lamb, one apiece for each household. If a family is too small for a whole lamb, it shall join the nearest household in procuring one and shall share in the lamb in proportion to the number of persons who partake of it. The lamb must be a year-old male and without blemish. You may take it from either the sheep or the goats. You shall keep it until the fourteenth day of this month, and then, with the whole assembly of Israel present, it shall be slaughtered during the evening twilight. They shall take some of its blood and apply it to the two doorposts and the lintel of every house in which they partake of the lamb. That same night they shall eat its roasted flesh with unleavened bread and bitter herbs. "This is how you are to eat it: with your loins girt, sandals on your feet and your staff in hand, you shall eat like those who are in flight. It is the Passover of the LORD. For on this same night I will go through Egypt, striking down every firstborn of the land, both man and beast, and executing judgment on all the gods of Egypt—I, the LORD! But the blood will mark the houses where you are. Seeing the blood, I will pass over you; thus, when I strike the land of Egypt, no destructive blow will come upon you. "This day shall be a memorial feast for you, which all your generations shall celebrate with pilgrimage to the LORD, as a perpetual institution."

Responsorial Psalm: Psalm 116:12-13, 15-16bc, 17-18
R. (1 Cor 10:16) Our blessing-cup is a communion with the Blood of Christ.

How shall I make a return to the LORD for all the good he has done for me? The cup of salvation I will take up, and I will call upon the name of the LORD. **R.**

Precious in the eyes of the LORD is the death of his faithful ones. I am your servant, the son of your handmaid; you have loosed my bonds. **R.**

To you will I offer sacrifice of thanksgiving, and I will call upon the name of the LORD. My vows to the LORD I will pay in the presence of all his people. **R.**

Second Reading: 1 Corinthians 11:23-26
Brothers and sisters: I received from the Lord what I also handed on to you, that the Lord Jesus, on the night he was handed over, took bread, and, after he had given thanks, broke it and said, "This is my body that is for you. Do this in remembrance of me." In the same way also the cup, after supper, saying, "This cup is the new covenant in my blood. Do this, as often as you drink it, in remembrance of me." For as often as you eat this bread and drink the cup, you proclaim the death of the Lord until he comes.

Verse before the Gospel: John 13:34
I give you a new commandment, says the Lord: love one another as I have loved you.

Gospel: John 13:1-15
Before the feast of Passover, Jesus knew that his hour had come to pass from this world to the Father. He loved his own in the world and he loved them to the end. The devil had already induced Judas, son of Simon the Iscariot, to hand him over. So, during supper, fully

aware that the Father had put everything into his power and that he had come from God and was returning to God, he rose from supper and took off his outer garments. He took a towel and tied it around his waist. Then he poured water into a basin and began to wash the disciples' feet and dry them with the towel around his waist. He came to Simon Peter, who said to him, "Master, are you going to wash my feet?" Jesus answered and said to him, "What I am doing, you do not understand now, but you will understand later." Peter said to him, "You will never wash my feet." Jesus answered him, "Unless I wash you, you will have no inheritance with me." Simon Peter said to him, "Master, then not only my feet, but my hands and head as well." Jesus said to him, "Whoever has bathed has no need except to have his feet washed, for he is clean all over; so you are clean, but not all." For he knew who would betray him; for this reason, he said, "Not all of you are clean." So when he had washed their feet and put his garments back on and reclined at table again, he said to them, "Do you realize what I have done for you? You call me 'teacher' and 'master,' and rightly so, for indeed I am. If I, therefore, the master and teacher, have washed your feet, you ought to wash one another's feet. I have given you a model to follow, so that as I have done for you, you should also do."

FRIDAY, APRIL 2
GOOD FRIDAY OF THE LORD'S PASSION
First Reading: Isaiah 52:13–53:12

See, my servant shall prosper, he shall be raised high and greatly exalted. Even as many were amazed at him so marred was his look beyond human semblance and his appearance beyond that of the sons of man so shall he startle many nations, because of him kings shall stand speechless; for those who have not been told shall see, those who have not heard shall ponder it. Who would believe what we have heard? To whom has the arm of the LORD been revealed? He grew up like a sapling before him, like a shoot from the parched earth; there was in him no stately bearing to make us look at him, nor appearance that would attract us to him. He was spurned and avoided by people, a man of suffering, accustomed to infirmity, one of those from whom people hide their faces, spurned, and we held him in no esteem. Yet it was our infirmities that he bore, our sufferings that he endured, while we thought of him as stricken, as one smitten by God and afflicted. But he was pierced for our offenses, crushed for our sins; upon him was the chastisement that makes us whole, by his stripes we were healed. We had all gone astray like sheep, each following his own way; but the LORD laid upon him the guilt of us all. Though he was harshly treated, he submitted and opened not his mouth; like a lamb led to the slaughter or a sheep before the shearers, he was silent and opened not his mouth. Oppressed and condemned, he was taken away, and who would have thought any more of his destiny? When he was cut off from the land of the living, and smitten for the sin of his people, a grave was assigned him among the wicked and a burial place with evildoers, though he had done no wrong nor spoken any falsehood. But the LORD was pleased to crush him in infirmity. If he gives his life as an offering for sin, he shall see his descendants in a long life, and the will of the LORD shall be accomplished through him. Because of his affliction he shall see the light in fullness of days; through his suffering, my servant shall justify many, and their guilt he shall bear. Therefore I will give him his portion among the great, and he shall divide the spoils with the mighty, because he surrendered himself to death and was counted among the wicked; and he shall take away the sins of many, and win pardon for their offenses.

Responsorial Psalm: Psalm 31:2, 6, 12-13, 15-16, 17, 25
R. (Lk 23:46) Father, into your hands I commend my spirit.
In you, O LORD, I take refuge; let me never be put to shame. In your justice rescue me. Into your hands I commend my spirit; you will redeem me, O LORD, O faithful God. **R.**
For all my foes I am an object of reproach, a laughingstock to my neighbors, and a dread to my friends; they who see me abroad flee

from me. I am forgotten like the unremembered dead; I am like a dish that is broken. **R**.

But my trust is in you, O LORD; I say, "You are my God. In your hands is my destiny; rescue me from the clutches of my enemies and my persecutors." **R**. Father, into your hands I commend my spirit. Let your face shine upon your servant; save me in your kindness. Take courage and be stouthearted, all you who hope in the LORD. **R**.

Second Reading: Hebrews 4:14-16; 5:7-9

Brothers and sisters: Since we have a great high priest who has passed through the heavens, Jesus, the Son of God, let us hold fast to our confession. For we do not have a high priest who is unable to sympathize with our weaknesses, but one who has similarly been tested in every way, yet without sin. So let us confidently approach the throne of grace to receive mercy and to find grace for timely help. In the days when Christ was in the flesh, he offered prayers and supplications with loud cries and tears to the one who was able to save him from death, and he was heard because of his reverence. Son though he was, he learned obedience from what he suffered; and when he was made perfect, he became the source of eternal salvation for all who obey him.

Verse before the Gospel: Philippians 2:8-9

Christ became obedient to the point of death, even death on a cross. Because of this, God greatly exalted him and bestowed on him the name which is above every other name.

Gospel: John 18:1-19:42

Jesus went out with his disciples across the Kidron valley to where there was a garden, into which he and his disciples entered. Judas his betrayer also knew the place, because Jesus had often met there with his disciples. So Judas got a band of soldiers and guards from the chief priests and the Pharisees and went there with lanterns, torches, and weapons. Jesus, knowing everything that was going to happen to him, went out and said to them, "Whom are you looking for?" They answered him, "Jesus the Nazorean." He said to them, "I AM." Judas his betrayer was also with them. When he said to them, "I AM, "they turned away and fell to the ground. So he again asked them, "Whom are you looking for?" They said, "Jesus the Nazorean." Jesus answered, "I told you that I AM. So if you are looking for me, let these men go." This was to fulfill what he had said, "I have not lost any of those you gave me." Then Simon Peter, who had a sword, drew it, struck the high priest's slave, and cut off his right ear. The slave's name was Malchus. Jesus said to Peter, "Put your sword into its scabbard. Shall I not drink the cup that the Father gave me?" So the band of soldiers, the tribune, and the Jewish guards seized Jesus, bound him, and brought him to Annas first. He was the father-in-law of Caiaphas, who was high priest that year. It was Caiaphas who had counseled the Jews that it was better that one man should die rather than the people. Simon Peter and another disciple followed Jesus. Now the other disciple was known to the high priest, and he entered the courtyard of the high priest with Jesus. But Peter stood at the gate outside. So the other disciple, the acquaintance of the high priest, went out and spoke to the gatekeeper and brought Peter in. Then the maid who was the gatekeeper said to Peter, "You are not one of this man's disciples, are you?" He said, "I am not." Now the slaves and the guards were standing around a charcoal fire that they had made, because it was cold, and were warming themselves. Peter was also standing there keeping warm. The high priest questioned Jesus about his disciples and about his doctrine. Jesus answered him, "I have spoken publicly to the world. I have always taught in a synagogue or in the temple area where all the Jews gather, and in secret I have said nothing. Why ask me? Ask those who heard me what I said to them. They know what I said." When he had said this, one of the temple guards standing there struck Jesus and said, "Is this the way you answer the high priest?" Jesus answered him, "If I have spoken wrongly, testify to the wrong; but if I have spoken rightly, why do you strike me?" Then Annas sent him bound to Caiaphas the high priest.

Now Simon Peter was standing there keeping warm. And they said to him, "You are not one of his disciples, are you?" He denied it and said, "I am not." One of the slaves of the high priest, a relative of the one whose ear Peter had cut off, said, "Didn't I see you in the garden with him?" Again Peter denied it. And immediately the cock crowed. Then they brought Jesus from Caiaphas to the praetorium. It was morning. And they themselves did not enter the praetorium, in order not to be defiled so that they could eat the Passover. So Pilate came out to them and said, "What charge do you bring against this man?" They answered and said to him, "If he were not a criminal, we would not have handed him over to you." At this, Pilate said to them, "Take him yourselves, and judge him according to your law." The Jews answered him, "We do not have the right to execute anyone, "in order that the word of Jesus might be fulfilled that he said indicating the kind of death he would die. So Pilate went back into the praetorium and summoned Jesus and said to him, "Are you the King of the Jews?" Jesus answered, "Do you say this on your own or have others told you about me?" Pilate answered, "I am not a Jew, am I? Your own nation and the chief priests handed you over to me. What have you done?" Jesus answered, "My kingdom does not belong to this world. If my kingdom did belong to this world, my attendants would be fighting to keep me from being handed over to the Jews. But as it is, my kingdom is not here." So Pilate said to him, "Then you are a king?" Jesus answered, "You say I am a king. For this I was born and for this I came into the world, to testify to the truth. Everyone who belongs to the truth listens to my voice." Pilate said to him, "What is truth?" When he had said this, he again went out to the Jews and said to them, "I find no guilt in him. But you have a custom that I release one prisoner to you at Passover. Do you want me to release to you the King of the Jews?" They cried out again, "Not this one but Barabbas!" Now Barabbas was a revolutionary. Then Pilate took Jesus and had him scourged. And the soldiers wove a crown out of thorns and placed it on his head, and clothed him in a purple cloak, and they came to him and said, "Hail, King of the Jews!" And they struck him repeatedly. Once more Pilate went out and said to them, "Look, I am bringing him out to you, so that you may know that I find no guilt in him." So Jesus came out, wearing the crown of thorns and the purple cloak. And he said to them, Behold, the man!" When the chief priests and the guards saw him they cried out, "Crucify him, crucify him!" Pilate said to them, "Take him yourselves and crucify him. I find no guilt in him." The Jews answered, "We have a law, and according to that law he ought to die, because he made himself the Son of God." Now when Pilate heard this statement, he became even more afraid, and went back into the praetorium and said to Jesus, "Where are you from?" Jesus did not answer him. So Pilate said to him, "Do you not speak to me? Do you not know that I have power to release you and I have power to crucify you?" Jesus answered him, "You would have no power over me if it had not been given to you from above. For this reason the one who handed me over to you has the greater sin." Consequently, Pilate tried to release him; but the Jews cried out, "If you release him, you are not a Friend of Caesar. Everyone who makes himself a king opposes Caesar."

When Pilate heard these words he brought Jesus out and seated him on the judge's bench in the place called Stone Pavement, in Hebrew, Gabbatha. It was preparation day for Passover, and it was about noon. And he said to the Jews, "Behold, your king!" They cried out, "Take him away, take him away! Crucify him!" Pilate said to them, "Shall I crucify your king?" The chief priests answered, "We have no king but Caesar." Then he handed him over to them to be crucified. So they took Jesus, and, carrying the cross himself, he went out to what is called the Place of the Skull, in Hebrew, Golgotha. There they crucified him, and with him two others, one on either side, with Jesus in the middle. Pilate also had an inscription written and put on the cross. It read, "Jesus the Nazorean, the King of the Jews." Now many of the Jews read this inscription, because the place where Jesus was crucified was near the city; and it was written in Hebrew, Latin, and Greek. So the chief priests of the Jews said to Pilate, "Do not write 'The King of the Jews,' but that he said, 'I am the King of the Jews'." Pilate answered, "What I have written, I have written."

When the soldiers had crucified Jesus, they took his clothes and divided them into four shares, a share for each soldier. They also took his tunic, but the tunic was seamless, woven in one piece from the top down. So they said to one another, "Let's not tear it, but cast lots for it to see whose it will be, " in order that the passage of Scripture might be fulfilled that says: *They divided my garments among them, and for my vesture they cast lots.* This is what the soldiers did.

Standing by the cross of Jesus were his mother and his mother's sister, Mary the wife of Clopas, and Mary of Magdala. When Jesus saw his mother and the disciple there whom he loved he said to his mother, "Woman, behold, your son." Then he said to the disciple, "Behold, your mother." And from that hour the disciple took her into his home. After this, aware that everything was now finished, in order that the Scripture might be fulfilled, Jesus said, "I thirst." There was a vessel filled with common wine. So they put a sponge soaked in wine on a sprig of hyssop and put it up to his mouth. When Jesus had taken the wine, he said, "It is finished." And bowing his head, he handed over the spirit.

Now since it was preparation day, in order that the bodies might not remain on the cross on the Sabbath, for the Sabbath day of that week was a solemn one, the Jews asked Pilate that their legs be broken and that they be taken down. So the soldiers came and broke the legs of the first and then of the other one who was crucified with Jesus. But when they came to Jesus and saw that he was already dead, they did not break his legs, but one soldier thrust his lance into his side, and immediately blood and water flowed out. An eyewitness has testified, and his testimony is true; he knows that he is speaking the truth, so that you also may come to believe. For this happened so that the Scripture passage might be fulfilled: *Not a bone of it will be broken.* And again another passage says: *They will look upon him whom they have pierced.*

After this, Joseph of Arimathea, secretly a disciple of Jesus for fear of the Jews, asked Pilate if he could remove the body of Jesus. And Pilate permitted it. So he came and took his body. Nicodemus, the one who had first come to him at night, also came bringing a mixture of myrrh and aloes weighing about one hundred pounds. They took the body of Jesus and bound it with burial cloths along with the spices, according to the Jewish burial custom. Now in the place where he had been crucified there was a garden, and in the garden a new tomb, in which no one had yet been buried. So they laid Jesus there because of the Jewish preparation day; for the tomb was close by.

SATURDAY, APRIL 3
HOLY SATURDAY
(At the Easter Vigil in the Holy Night of Easter)
First Reading: Genesis 1:1-2:2 or 1:1, 26-31a

In the beginning, when God created the heavens and the earth, the earth was a formless wasteland, and darkness covered the abyss, while a mighty wind swept over the waters. Then God said, "Let there be light," and there was light. God saw how good the light was. God then separated the light from the darkness. God called the light "day," and the darkness he called "night." Thus evening came, and morning followed—the first day.

Then God said, "Let there be a dome in the middle of the waters, to separate one body of water from the other." And so it happened: God made the dome, and it separated the water above the dome from the water below it. God called the dome "the sky." Evening came, and morning followed—the second day.

Then God said, "Let the water under the sky be gathered into a single basin, so that the dry land may appear." And so it happened: the water under the sky was gathered into its basin, and the dry land appeared. God called the dry land "the earth," and the basin of the water he called "the sea." God saw how good it was. Then God said, "Let the earth bring forth vegetation: every kind of plant that bears seed and every kind of fruit tree on earth that bears fruit with its seed in it." And so it happened: the earth brought forth every kind of plant that bears seed and every kind of fruit tree on earth that bears fruit with its seed in it. God saw how good it was. Evening came, and morning followed—the third day.

Then God said: "Let there be lights in the dome of the sky, to separate day from night. Let them mark the fixed times, the days and the years, and serve as luminaries in the dome of the sky, to shed light upon the earth." And so it happened: God made the two great lights, the greater one to govern the day, and the lesser one to govern the night; and he made the stars. God set them in the dome of the sky, to shed light upon the earth, to govern the day and the night, and to separate the light from the darkness. God saw how good it was. Evening came, and morning followed—the fourth day.

Then God said, "Let the water teem with an abundance of living creatures, and on the earth let birds fly beneath the dome of the sky." And so it happened: God created the great sea monsters and all kinds of swimming creatures with which the water teems, and all kinds of winged birds. God saw how good it was, and God blessed them, saying, "Be fertile, multiply, and fill the water of the seas; and let the birds multiply on the earth." Evening came, and morning followed—the fifth day.

Then God said, "Let the earth bring forth all kinds of living creatures: cattle, creeping things, and wild animals of all kinds." And so it happened: God made all kinds of wild animals, all kinds of cattle, and all kinds of creeping things of the earth. God saw how good it was. Then God said: "Let us make man in our image, after our likeness. Let them have dominion over the fish of the sea, the birds of the air, and the cattle, and over all the wild animals and all the creatures that crawl on the ground." God created man in his image; in the image of God he created him; male and female he created them. God blessed them, saying: "Be fertile and multiply; fill the earth and subdue it. Have dominion over the fish of the sea, the birds of the air, and all the living things that move on the earth." God also said: "See, I give you every seed-bearing plant all over the earth and every tree that has seed-bearing fruit on it to be your food; and to all the animals of the land, all the birds of the air, and all the living creatures that crawl on the ground, I give all the green plants for food." And so it happened. God looked at everything he had made, and he found it very good. Evening came, and morning followed— the sixth day. Thus the heavens and the earth and all their array were completed.

Since on the seventh day God was finished with the work he had been doing, he rested on the seventh day from all the work he had undertaken.

Or:

Genesis 1:1, 26-31a

In the beginning, when God created the heavens and the earth, God said: "Let us make man in our image, after our likeness. Let them have dominion over the fish of the sea, the birds of the air, and the cattle, and over all the wild animals and all the creatures that crawl on the ground." God created man in his image; in the image of God he created him; male and female he created them. God blessed them, saying: "Be fertile and multiply; fill the earth and subdue it. Have dominion over the fish of the sea, the birds of the air, and all the living things that move on the earth." God also said: "See, I give you every seed-bearing plant all over the earth and every tree that has seed-bearing fruit on it to be your food; and to all the animals of the land, all the birds of the air, and all the living creatures that crawl on the ground, I give all the green plants for food." And so it happened. God looked at everything he had made, and found it very good.

Responsorial Psalm: Psalm 104:1-2, 5-6, 10, 12, 13-14, 24, 35

R. (30) Lord, send out your Spirit, and renew the face of the earth.

Bless the LORD, O my soul! O LORD, my God, you are great indeed! You are clothed with majesty and glory, robed in light as with a cloak. **R.**

You fixed the earth upon its foundation, not to be moved forever; with the ocean, as with a garment, you covered it; above the mountains the waters stood. **R.**

You send forth springs into the watercourses that wind among the mountains. Beside them the birds of heaven dwell; from among the branches they send forth their song. **R.**

You water the mountains from your palace; the earth is replete with the fruit of your works. You raise grass for the cattle, and vegetation for man's use, Producing bread from the earth. **R.**

How manifold are your works, O LORD! In wisdom you have wrought them all—the earth is full of your creatures. Bless the LORD, O my soul! **R.**

Or:
Psalm 33:4-5, 6-7, 12-13, 20 and 22
R. (5b) The earth is full of the goodness of the Lord.

Upright is the word of the LORD, and all his works are trustworthy. He loves justice and right; of the kindness of the LORD the earth is full. **R.**

By the word of the LORD the heavens were made; by the breath of his mouth all their host. He gathers the waters of the sea as in a flask; in cellars he confines the deep. **R.**

Blessed the nation whose God is the LORD, the people he has chosen for his own inheritance. From heaven the LORD looks down; he sees all mankind. **R.**

Our soul waits for the LORD, who is our help and our shield. May your kindness, O LORD, be upon us who have put our hope in you. **R.**

Second Reading: Genesis 22:1-18 or 22:1-2, 9a, 10-13, 15-18

God put Abraham to the test. He called to him, "Abraham!" "Here I am," he replied. Then God said: "Take your son Isaac, your only one, whom you love, and go to the land of Moriah. There you shall offer him up as a holocaust on a height that I will point out to you." Early the next morning Abraham saddled his donkey, took with him his son Isaac and two of his servants as well, and with the wood that he had cut for the holocaust, set out for the place of which God had told him.

On the third day Abraham got sight of the place from afar. Then he said to his servants: "Both of you stay here with the donkey, while the boy and I go on over yonder. We will worship and then come back to you." Thereupon Abraham took the wood for the holocaust and laid it on his son Isaac's shoulders, while he himself carried the fire and the knife. As the two walked on together, Isaac spoke to his father Abraham: "Father!" Isaac said. "Yes, son," he replied. Isaac continued, "Here are the fire and the wood, but where is the sheep for the holocaust?" "Son," Abraham answered, "God himself will provide the sheep for the holocaust." Then the two continued going forward. When they came to the place of which God had told him, Abraham built an altar there and arranged the wood on it. Next he tied up his son Isaac, and put him on top of the wood on the altar. Then he reached out and took the knife to slaughter his son. But the LORD's messenger called to him from heaven, "Abraham, Abraham!" "Here I am!" he answered. "Do not lay your hand on the boy," said the messenger. "Do not do the least thing to him. I know now how devoted you are to God, since you did not withhold from me your own beloved son." As Abraham looked about, he spied a ram caught by its horns in the thicket. So he went and took the ram and offered it up as a holocaust in place of his son. Abraham named the site Yahweh-yireh; hence people now say, "On the mountain the LORD will see." Again the LORD's messenger called to Abraham from heaven and said: "I swear by myself, declares the LORD, that because you acted as you did in not withholding from me your beloved son, I will bless you abundantly and make your descendants as countless as the stars of the sky and the sands of the seashore; your descendants shall take possession of the gates of their enemies, and in your descendants all the nations of the earth shall find blessing-- all this because you obeyed my command."

Or:
Genesis 22:1-2, 9a, 10-13, 15-18
God put Abraham to the test. He called to him, "Abraham!" "Here I am," he replied. Then God said: "Take your son Isaac, your only one, whom you love, and go to the land of Moriah. There you shall offer him up as a holocaust on a height that I will point out to you."

When they came to the place of which God had told him, Abraham built an altar there and arranged the wood on it. Then he reached out and took the knife to slaughter his son. But the LORD's messenger called to him from heaven, "Abraham, Abraham!" "Here I am," he answered. "Do not lay your hand on the boy," said the messenger. "Do not do the least thing to him. I know now how devoted you are to God, since you did not withhold from me your own beloved son." As Abraham looked about, he spied a ram caught by its horns in the thicket. So he went and took the ram and offered it up as a holocaust in place of his son.

Again the LORD's messenger called to Abraham from heaven and said: "I swear by myself, declares the LORD, that because you acted as you did in not withholding from me your beloved son, I will bless you abundantly and make your descendants as countless as the stars of the sky and the sands of the seashore; your descendants shall take possession of the gates of their enemies, and in your descendants all the nations of the earth shall find blessing-- all this because you obeyed my command."

Responsorial Psalm: Psalm 16:5, 8, 9-10, 11
R. (1) You are my inheritance, O Lord.
O LORD, my allotted portion and my cup, you it is who hold fast my lot. I set the LORD ever before me; with him at my right hand I shall not be disturbed. **R.**

Therefore my heart is glad and my soul rejoices, my body, too, abides in confidence; because you will not abandon my soul to the netherworld, nor will you suffer your faithful one to undergo corruption. **R**.

You will show me the path to life, fullness of joys in your presence, the delights at your right hand forever. **R**.

Third Reading: Exodus 14:15-15:1

The LORD said to Moses, "Why are you crying out to me? Tell the Israelites to go forward. And you, lift up your staff and, with hand outstretched over the sea, split the sea in two, that the Israelites may pass through it on dry land. But I will make the Egyptians so obstinate that they will go in after them. Then I will receive glory through Pharaoh and all his army, his chariots and charioteers. The Egyptians shall know that I am the LORD, when I receive glory through Pharaoh and his chariots and charioteers." The angel of God, who had been leading Israel's camp, now moved and went around behind them. The column of cloud also, leaving the front, took up its place behind them, so that it came between the camp of the Egyptians and that of Israel. But the cloud now became dark, and thus the night passed without the rival camps coming any closer together all night long. Then Moses stretched out his hand over the sea, and the LORD swept the sea with a strong east wind throughout the night and so turned it into dry land. When the water was thus divided, the Israelites marched into the midst of the sea on dry land, with the water like a wall to their right and to their left.

The Egyptians followed in pursuit; all Pharaoh's horses and chariots and charioteers went after them right into the midst of the sea. In the night watch just before dawn the LORD cast through the column of the fiery cloud upon the Egyptian force a glance that threw it into a panic; and he so clogged their chariot wheels that they could hardly drive. With that the Egyptians sounded the retreat before Israel, because the LORD was fighting for them against the Egyptians. Then the LORD told Moses, "Stretch out your hand over the sea, that the water may flow back upon the Egyptians, upon their chariots and their charioteers." So Moses stretched out his hand over the sea, and at dawn the sea flowed back to its normal depth. The Egyptians were fleeing head on toward the sea, when the LORD hurled them into its midst. As the water flowed back, it covered the chariots and the charioteers of Pharaoh's whole army which had followed the Israelites into the sea. Not a single one of them escaped. But the Israelites had marched on dry land through the midst of the sea, with the water like a wall to their right and to their left. Thus the LORD saved Israel on that day from the power of the Egyptians. When Israel saw the Egyptians lying dead on the seashore and beheld the great power that the LORD had shown against the Egyptians, they feared the LORD and believed in him and in his servant Moses. Then Moses and the Israelites sang this song to the LORD: I will sing to the LORD, for he is gloriously triumphant; horse and chariot he has cast into the sea.

Responsorial Psalm: Exodus 15:1-2, 3-4, 5-6, 17-18
R. (1b) Let us sing to the Lord; he has covered himself in glory.
I will sing to the LORD, for he is gloriously triumphant; horse and chariot he has cast into the sea. My strength and my courage is the LORD, and he has been my savior. He is my God, I praise him; the God of my father, I extol him. **R.**

The LORD is a warrior, LORD is his name! Pharaoh's chariots and army he hurled into the sea; the elite of his officers were submerged in the Red Sea. **R.**

The flood waters covered them, they sank into the depths like a stone. Your right hand, O LORD, magnificent in power, your right hand, O LORD, has shattered the enemy. **R.**

You brought in the people you redeemed and planted them on the mountain of your inheritance the place where you made your seat, O LORD, the sanctuary, LORD, which your hands established. The LORD shall reign forever and ever. **R.**

Fourth Reading: Isaiah 54:5-14
The One who has become your husband is your Maker; his name is

the LORD of hosts; your redeemer is the Holy One of Israel, called God of all the earth. The LORD calls you back, like a wife forsaken and grieved in spirit, a wife married in youth and then cast off, says your God. For a brief moment I abandoned you, but with great tenderness I will take you back. In an outburst of wrath, for a moment I hid my face from you; but with enduring love I take pity on you, says the LORD, your redeemer. This is for me like the days of Noah, when I swore that the waters of Noah should never again deluge the earth; so I have sworn not to be angry with you, or to rebuke you. Though the mountains leave their place and the hills be shaken, my love shall never leave you nor my covenant of peace be shaken, says the LORD, who has mercy on you. O afflicted one, storm-battered and unconsoled, I lay your pavements in carnelians, and your foundations in sapphires; I will make your battlements of rubies, your gates of carbuncles, and all your walls of precious stones. All your children shall be taught by the LORD, and great shall be the peace of your children. In justice shall you be established, far from the fear of oppression, where destruction cannot come near you.

Responsorial Psalm: Psalm 30:2, 4, 5-6, 11-12, 13
R. (2a) I will praise you, Lord, for you have rescued me.
I will extol you, O LORD, for you drew me clear and did not let my enemies rejoice over me. O LORD, you brought me up from the netherworld; you preserved me from among those going down into the pit. **R.**

Sing praise to the LORD, you his faithful ones, and give thanks to his holy name. For his anger lasts but a moment; a lifetime, his good will. At nightfall, weeping enters in, but with the dawn, rejoicing. **R.**

Hear, O LORD, and have pity on me; O LORD, be my helper. You changed my mourning into dancing; O LORD, my God, forever will I give you thanks. **R.**

Fifth Reading: Isaiah 55:1-11
Thus says the LORD: All you who are thirsty, come to the water!

You who have no money, come, receive grain and eat; come, without paying and without cost, drink wine and milk! Why spend your money for what is not bread, your wages for what fails to satisfy? Heed me, and you shall eat well, you shall delight in rich fare. Come to me heedfully, listen, that you may have life. I will renew with you the everlasting covenant, the benefits assured to David. As I made him a witness to the peoples, a leader and commander of nations, so shall you summon a nation you knew not, and nations that knew you not shall run to you, because of the LORD, your God, the Holy One of Israel, who has glorified you. Seek the LORD while he may be found, call him while he is near. Let the scoundrel forsake his way, and the wicked man his thoughts; let him turn to the LORD for mercy; to our God, who is generous in forgiving. For my thoughts are not your thoughts, nor are your ways my ways, says the LORD. As high as the heavens are above the earth, so high are my ways above your ways and my thoughts above your thoughts. For just as from the heavens the rain and snow come down and do not return there till they have watered the earth, making it fertile and fruitful, giving seed to the one who sows and bread to the one who eats, so shall my word be that goes forth from my mouth; my word shall not return to me void, but shall do my will, achieving the end for which I sent it.

Responsorial Psalm: Isaiah 12:2-3, 4, 5-6
R. (3) You will draw water joyfully from the springs of salvation.
God indeed is my savior; I am confident and unafraid. My strength and my courage is the LORD, and he has been my savior. With joy you will draw water at the fountain of salvation. **R.**
Give thanks to the LORD, acclaim his name; among the nations make known his deeds, proclaim how exalted is his name. **R.**
Sing praise to the LORD for his glorious achievement; let this be known throughout all the earth. Shout with exultation, O city of Zion, for great in your midst is the Holy One of Israel! **R.**

Sixth Reading: Baruch 3:9-15, 32-4:4

Hear, O Israel, the commandments of life: Listen, and know prudence! How is it, Israel, that you are in the land of your foes, grown old in a foreign land, defiled with the dead, accounted with those destined for the netherworld? You have forsaken the fountain of wisdom! Had you walked in the way of God, you would have dwelt in enduring peace. Learn where prudence is, where strength, where understanding; that you may know also where are length of days, and life, where light of the eyes, and peace. Who has found the place of wisdom, who has entered into her treasuries? The One who knows all things knows her; he has probed her by his knowledge— The One who established the earth for all time, and filled it with four-footed beasts; he who dismisses the light, and it departs, calls it, and it obeys him trembling; before whom the stars at their posts shine and rejoice; when he calls them, they answer, "Here we are!" shining with joy for their Maker. Such is our God; no other is to be compared to him: he has traced out the whole way of understanding, and has given her to Jacob, his servant, to Israel, his beloved son. Since then she has appeared on earth, and moved among people. She is the book of the precepts of God, the law that endures forever; all who cling to her will live, but those will die who forsake her. Turn, O Jacob, and receive her: walk by her light toward splendor. Give not your glory to another, your privileges to an alien race. Blessed are we, O Israel; for what pleases God is known to us!

Responsorial Psalm: Psalm 19:8, 9, 10, 11
R. (John 6:68c) Lord, you have the words of everlasting life.
The law of the LORD is perfect, refreshing the soul; the decree of the LORD is trustworthy, giving wisdom to the simple. **R.**
The precepts of the LORD are right, rejoicing the heart; the command of the LORD is clear, enlightening the eye. **R.**
The fear of the LORD is pure, enduring forever; the ordinances of the LORD are true, all of them just. **R.**
They are more precious than gold, than a heap of purest gold;

sweeter also than syrup or honey from the comb. **R.**

Seventh Reading: Ezra 36:16-17a, 18-28

The word of the LORD came to me, saying: Son of man, when the house of Israel lived in their land, they defiled it by their conduct and deeds. Therefore I poured out my fury upon them because of the blood that they poured out on the ground, and because they defiled it with idols. I scattered them among the nations, dispersing them over foreign lands; according to their conduct and deeds I judged them. But when they came among the nations wherever they came, they served to profane my holy name, because it was said of them: "These are the people of the LORD, yet they had to leave their land." So I have relented because of my holy name which the house of Israel profaned among the nations where they came. Therefore say to the house of Israel: Thus says the Lord GOD: Not for your sakes do I act, house of Israel, but for the sake of my holy name, which you profaned among the nations to which you came. I will prove the holiness of my great name, profaned among the nations, in whose midst you have profaned it. Thus the nations shall know that I am the LORD, says the Lord GOD, when in their sight I prove my holiness through you. For I will take you away from among the nations, gather you from all the foreign lands, and bring you back to your own land. I will sprinkle clean water upon you to cleanse you from all your impurities, and from all your idols I will cleanse you. I will give you a new heart and place a new spirit within you, taking from your bodies your stony hearts and giving you natural hearts. I will put my spirit within you and make you live by my statutes, careful to observe my decrees. You shall live in the land I gave your fathers; you shall be my people, and I will be your God.

Responsorial Psalm: Psalm 42:3, 5; 43:3, 4

[*When baptism is celebrated.*]

R. (42:2) Like a deer that longs for running streams, my soul longs for you, my God.

Athirst is my soul for God, the living God. When shall I go and behold the face of God? **R**

I went with the throng and led them in procession to the house of God, amid loud cries of joy and thanksgiving, with the multitude keeping festival. **R.**

Send forth your light and your fidelity; they shall lead me on and bring me to your holy mountain, to your dwelling-place. **R.**

Then will I go in to the altar of God, the God of my gladness and joy; then will I give you thanks upon the harp, O God, my God! **R.**

Or:
Isaiah 12:2-3, 4bcd, 5-6
[When baptism is not celebrated.]

R. (3) You will draw water joyfully from the springs of salvation.

God indeed is my savior; I am confident and unafraid. My strength and my courage is the LORD, and he has been my savior. With joy you will draw water at the fountain of salvation. **R.**

Give thanks to the LORD, acclaim his name; among the nations make known his deeds, proclaim how exalted is his name. **R.**

Sing praise to the LORD for his glorious achievement; let this be known throughout all the earth. Shout with exultation, O city of Zion, for great in your midst is the Holy One of Israel! **R.**

Or:
Psalm 51:12-13, 14-15, 18-19
[When baptism is not celebrated.]

R. (12a) Create a clean heart in me, O God.

A clean heart create for me, O God, and a steadfast spirit renew within me. Cast me not out from your presence, and your Holy Spirit take not from me. **R.**

Give me back the joy of your salvation, and a willing spirit sustain in me. I will teach transgressors your ways, and sinners shall return to you. **R.**

For you are not pleased with sacrifices; should I offer a holocaust, you would not accept it. My sacrifice, O God, is a contrite spirit; a heart contrite and humbled, O God, you will not spurn. **R**.

Epistle: Romans 6:3-11

Brothers and sisters: Are you unaware that we who were baptized into Christ Jesus were baptized into his death? We were indeed buried with him through baptism into death, so that, just as Christ was raised from the dead by the glory of the Father, we too might live in newness of life. For if we have grown into union with him through a death like his, we shall also be united with him in the resurrection. We know that our old self was crucified with him, so that our sinful body might be done away with, that we might no longer be in slavery to sin. For a dead person has been absolved from sin. If, then, we have died with Christ, we believe that we shall also live with him. We know that Christ, raised from the dead, dies no more; death no longer has power over him. As to his death, he died to sin once and for all; as to his life, he lives for God. Consequently, you too must think of yourselves as being dead to sin and living for God in Christ Jesus.

Responsorial Psalm: Psalm 118:1-2, 16-17, 22-23
R. Alleluia, alleluia, alleluia.

Give thanks to the LORD, for he is good, for his mercy endures forever. Let the house of Israel say, "His mercy endures forever." **R**.
The right hand of the LORD has struck with power; the right hand of the LORD is exalted. I shall not die, but live, and declare the works of the LORD. **R**.
The stone the builders rejected has become the cornerstone. By the LORD has this been done; it is wonderful in our eyes. **R**.

Gospel: Mark 16:1-7

When the Sabbath was over, Mary Magdalene, Mary, the mother of James, and Salome bought spices so that they might go and anoint him. Very early when the sun had risen, on the first day of the week, they came to the tomb. They were saying to one another, "Who will roll back the stone for us from the entrance to the tomb? When they looked up, they saw that the stone had been rolled back; it was very large. On entering the tomb they saw a young man sitting on the right side, clothed in a white robe, and they were utterly amazed. He said to them, "Do not be amazed! You seek Jesus of Nazareth, the crucified. He has been raised; he is not here. Behold the place where they laid him. But go and tell his disciples and Peter, 'He is going before you to Galilee; there you will see him, as he told you.'"

SUNDAY, APRIL 4
EASTER SUNDAY
THE RESURRECTION OF THE LORD

First Reading: Acts 10:34a, 37-43

Peter proceeded to speak and said: "You know what has happened all over Judea, beginning in Galilee after the baptism that John preached, how God anointed Jesus of Nazareth with the Holy Spirit and power. He went about doing good and healing all those oppressed by the devil, for God was with him. We are witnesses of all that he did both in the country of the Jews and in Jerusalem. They put him to death by hanging him on a tree. This man God raised on the third day and granted that he be visible, not to all the people, but to us, the witnesses chosen by God in advance, who ate and drank with him after he rose from the dead. He commissioned us to preach to the people and testify that he is the one appointed by God as judge of the living and the dead. To him all the prophets bear witness, that everyone who believes in him will receive forgiveness of sins through his name."

Responsorial Psalm: Psalm 118:1-2, 16-17, 22-23
R. (24) This is the day the Lord has made; let us rejoice and be glad.
Or:
R. Alleluia.

Give thanks to the LORD, for he is good, for his mercy endures forever. Let the house of Israel say, "His mercy endures forever." **R.**
"The right hand of the LORD has struck with power; the right hand of the LORD is exalted. I shall not die, but live, and declare the works of the LORD." **R.**
The stone which the builders rejected has become the cornerstone. By the LORD has this been done; it is wonderful in our eyes. **R.**

Second Reading: Colossians 3:1-4 or 1 Corinthians 5:6b-8

Brothers and sisters: If then you were raised with Christ, seek what is above, where Christ is seated at the right hand of God. Think of what is above, not of what is on earth. For you have died, and your life is hidden with Christ in God. When Christ your life appears, then you too will appear with him in glory.

Or:

1 Corinthians 5:6b-8

Brothers and sisters: Do you not know that a little yeast leavens all the dough? Clear out the old yeast, so that you may become a fresh batch of dough, inasmuch as you are unleavened. For our paschal lamb, Christ, has been sacrificed. Therefore, let us celebrate the feast, not with the old yeast, the yeast of malice and wickedness, but with the unleavened bread of sincerity and truth.

Sequence: Victimae Paschali Laudes

Christians, to the Paschal Victim
Offer your thankful praises!
A Lamb the sheep redeems;
Christ, who only is sinless,
Reconciles sinners to the Father.
Death and life have contended in that combat stupendous:
The Prince of life, who died, reigns immortal.
Speak, Mary, declaring
What you saw, wayfaring.

"The tomb of Christ, who is living,
The glory of Jesus' resurrection;
bright angels attesting,
The shroud and napkin resting.
Yes, Christ my hope is arisen;
to Galilee he goes before you."
Christ indeed from death is risen, our new life obtaining.
Have mercy, victor King, ever reigning!
Amen. Alleluia.

Alleluia: 1 Corinthian 5:7b-8a
R. Alleluia, alleluia.
Christ, our paschal lamb, has been sacrificed; let us then feast with
joy in the Lord. **R.**

Gospel: John 20:1-9
On the first day of the week, Mary of Magdala came to the tomb
early in the morning, while it was still dark, and saw the stone
removed from the tomb. So she ran and went to Simon Peter and to
the other disciple whom Jesus loved, and told them, "They have
taken the Lord from the tomb, and we don't know where they put
him." So Peter and the other disciple went out and came to the tomb.
They both ran, but the other disciple ran faster than Peter and arrived
at the tomb first; he bent down and saw the burial cloths there, but
did not go in. When Simon Peter arrived after him, he went into the
tomb and saw the burial cloths there, and the cloth that had covered
his head, not with the burial cloths but rolled up in a separate place.
Then the other disciple also went in, the one who had arrived at the
tomb first, and he saw and believed. For they did not yet understand
the Scripture that he had to rise from the dead.

STATIONS OF THE CROSS

The presiding minister may be a priest, deacon, or layperson. This minister prays the opening and closing prayers, leads the acclamation, announces the stations, and says the prayer that concludes each station. One or more readers may read the Scriptural reflections. A period of silence should be observed between the Scripture reading and the prayer. A cross bearer accompanied by two candle bearers may stand in front of each station as it is announced.

BEFORE EACH STATION:

Minister:

We adore you, O Christ, and we bless you.

All:

Because by your holy cross you have redeemed the world.

AFTER EACH STATION:

All:

Lord Jesus, help us walk in your steps.

OPENING PRAYER:

Minister:

God of power and mercy, in love you sent your Son that we might be cleansed of sin and live with you forever. Bless us as we gather to reflect on his suffering and death that we may learn from his example the way we should go. We ask this through that same Christ, our Lord.

All:

Amen.

FIRST STATION: JESUS IN THE GARDEN OF GETHSEMANE

Reader:

Then Jesus came with them to a place called Gethsemane, and he said to his disciples, "Sit here while I go over there and pray." He took along Peter and the two sons of Zebedee, and began to feel sorrow and distress. Then he said to them, "My soul is sorrowful even to death. Remain here and keep watch with me." He advanced a little and fell prostrate in prayer, saying, "My Father, if it is possible, let this cup pass from me; yet, not as I will, but as you will." When he returned to his disciples he found them asleep. He said to Peter, "So you could not keep watch with me for one hour? Watch and pray that you may not undergo the test. The spirit is willing, but the flesh is weak."

(Matthew 26:36-41)

Minister:

Lord, grant us your strength and wisdom, that we may seek to follow your will in all things

SECOND STATION: JESUS, BETRAYED BY JUDAS, IS ARRESTED

Reader:

Then, while [Jesus] was still speaking, Judas, one of the Twelve, arrived, accompanied by a crowd with swords and clubs, who had come from the chief priests, the scribes, and the elders. His betrayer had arranged a signal with them, saying, "The man I shall kiss is the one; arrest him and lead him away securely." He came and immediately went over to him and said, "Rabbi." And he kissed him. At this they laid hands on him and arrested him.

(Mark 14: 43-46)

Minister:

Lord, grant us the courage of our convictions that our lives may faithfully reflect the good news you bring.

THIRD STATION: JESUS IS CONDEMNED BY THE SANHEDRIN

Reader:

When day came the council of elders of the people met, both chief priests and scribes, and they brought him before their Sanhedrin.

They said, "If you are the Messiah, tell us," but he replied to them, "If I tell you, you will not believe, and if I question, you will not respond. But from this time on the Son of Man will be seated at the right hand of the power of God." They all asked, "Are you then the Son of God?" He replied to them, "You say that I am." Then they said, "What further need have we for testimony? We have heard it from his own mouth."

(Luke 22: 66-71)

Minister:

Lord, grant us your sense of righteousness that we may never cease to work to bring about the justice of the kingdom that you promised.

FOURTH STATION: JESUS IS DENIED BY PETER
Reader:

Now Peter was sitting outside in the courtyard. One of the maids came over to him and said, "You too were with Jesus the Galilean." But he denied it in front of everyone, saying, "I do not know what you are talking about!" As he went out to the gate, another girl saw him and said to those who were there, "This man was with Jesus the Nazorean." Again he denied it with an oath, "I do not know the man!" A little later the bystanders came over and said to Peter, "Surely you too are one of them; even your speech gives you away." At that he began to curse and to swear, "I do not know the man." And immediately a cock crowed. Then Peter remembered the word that Jesus had spoken: "Before the cock crows you will deny me three times." He went out and began to weep bitterly.

(Matthew 26: 69-75)

Minister:

Lord, grant us the gift of honesty that we may not fear to speak the truth even when difficult.

FIFTH STATION: JESUS IS JUDGED BY PILATE
Reader:

The chief priests with the elders and the scribes, that is, the whole

Sanhedrin, held a council. They bound Jesus, led him away, and handed him over to Pilate. Pilate questioned him, "Are you the king of the Jews?" He said to him in reply, "You say so." The chief priests accused him of many things. Again Pilate questioned him, "Have you no answer? See how many things they accuse you of." Jesus gave him no further answer, so that Pilate was amazed.... Pilate, wishing to satisfy the crowd, released Barrabas... [and] handed [Jesus] over to be crucified.

(Mark 15: 1-5, 15)

Minister:

Lord, grant us discernment that we may see as you see, not as the world sees.

SIXTH STATION: JESUS IS SCOURGED AND CROWNED WITH THORNS

Reader:

Then Pilate took Jesus and had him scourged. And the soldiers wove a crown out of thorns and placed it on his head, and clothed him in a purple cloak, and they came to him and said, "Hail, King of the Jews!" And they struck him repeatedly.

(John 19: 1-3)

Minister:

Lord, grant us patience in times of suffering that we may offer our lives as a sacrifice of praise.

SEVENTH STATION: JESUS BEARS THE CROSS

Reader:

When the chief priests and the guards saw [Jesus] they cried out, "Crucify him, crucify him!" Pilate said to them, "Take him yourselves and crucify him. I find no guilt in him."... They cried out, "Take him away, take him away! Crucify him!" Pilate said to them, "Shall I crucify your king?" The chief priests answered, "We have no king but Caesar." Then he handed him over to them to be crucified. So they

took Jesus, and carrying the cross himself he went out to what is called the Place of the Skull, in Hebrew, Golgotha.
(John 19: 6, 15-17)

Lord, grant us strength of purpose that we may faithfully bear our crosses each day.

EIGHTH STATION: JESUS IS HELPED BY SIMON THE CYRENIAN TO CARRY THE CROSS

Reader:

They pressed into service a passer-by, Simon, a Cyrenian, who was coming in from the country, the father of Alexander and Rufus, to carry his cross.
(Mark 15: 21)

Lord, grant us willing spirits that we may be your instruments on earth.

NINTH STATION: JESUS MEETS THE WOMEN OF JERUSALEM

Reader:

A large crowd of people followed Jesus, including many women who mourned and lamented him. Jesus turned to them and said, "Daughters of Jerusalem, do not weep for me; weep instead for yourselves and for your children, for indeed, the days are coming when people will say, 'Blessed are the barren, the wombs that never bore and the breasts that never nursed.' At that time, people will say to the mountains, 'Fall upon us!' and to the hills, 'Cover us!' for if these things are done when the wood is green what will happen when it is dry?"
(Luke 23: 27-31)

Lord, grant us gentle spirits that we may comfort those who mourn.

TENTH STATION: JESUS IS CRUCIFIED

Reader:

When they came to the place called the Skull, they crucified him and the criminals there, one on his right, the other on his left. [Then Jesus said, "Father, forgive them, they know not what they do."]

(Luke 23: 33-34)

Minister:

Lord, grant us merciful hearts that we may bring your reconciliation and forgiveness to all.

ELEVENTH STATION: JESUS PROMISES HIS KINGDOM TO THE GOOD THIEF

Reader:

Now one of the criminals hanging there reviled Jesus, saying, "Are you not the Messiah? Save yourself and us." The other, however, rebuking him, said in reply, "Have you no fear of God, for you are subject to the same condemnation? And indeed, we have been condemned justly, for the sentence we received corresponds to our crimes, but this man has done nothing criminal." Then he said, "Jesus, remember me when you come into your kingdom." He replied to him, "Amen, I say to you, today you will be with me in Paradise."

(Luke 23: 39-43)

Minister:

Lord, grant us perseverance that we may never stop seeking you.

TWELFTH STATION: JESUS SPEAKS TO HIS MOTHER AND THE DISCIPLE

Reader:

Standing by the cross of Jesus were his mother and his mother's sister, Mary the wife of Clopas, and Mary of Magdala. When Jesus saw his mother and the disciple there whom he loved, he said to his mother, "Woman, behold, your son." Then he said to the disciple, "Behold, your mother." And from that hour the disciple took her into his home.

John 19: 25-27
Minister:
Lord, grant us constancy that we may be willing to stand by those in need.

THIRTEENTH STATION: JESUS DIES ON THE CROSS
Reader:
It was now about noon and darkness came over the whole land until three in the afternoon because of an eclipse of the sun. Then the veil of the temple was torn down the middle. Jesus cried out in a loud voice, "Father, into your hands I commend my spirit"; and when he had said this he breathed his last.
(Luke 23: 44-46)
Minister:
Lord, grant us trust in you that when our time on earth in ended our spirits may come to you without delay.

FOURTEENTH STATION: JESUS IS PLACED IN THE TOMB
Reader:
When it was evening, there came a rich man from Arimathea named Joseph, who was himself a disciple of Jesus. He went to Pilate and asked for the body of Jesus; then Pilate ordered it to be handed over. Taking the body, Joseph wrapped it [in] clean linen and laid it in his new tomb that he had hewn in the rock. Then he rolled a huge stone across the entrance to the tomb and departed.
(Matthew 27: 57-60)
Minister:
Lord, grant us your compassion that we may always provide for those in need.

CLOSING PRAYER:
Minister:
Lord Jesus Christ, your passion and death is the sacrifice that unites earth and heaven and reconciles all people to you. May we who have

faithfully reflected on these mysteries follow in your steps and so come to share your glory in heaven where you live and reign with the Father and the Holy Spirit one God, forever and ever.

All:

Amen.

CATHOLIC PRAYERS

God invites us into a relationship with Him that is both personal and communal. He speaks to us through His Son, Jesus Christ - the Word-made-flesh. Prayer is our response to God who is already speaking or, better yet, revealing Himself to us. Therefore, prayer is not merely an exchange of words, but it engages the whole person in a relationship with God the Father, through the Son, and in the Holy Spirit.

This section includes some of the most familiar prayers of the Catholic tradition. They include basic prayers, which you may wish to learn by heart so that they become part of your daily living.

OUR FATHER

Our Father who art in heaven,
Hallowed be thy name.
Thy kingdom come.
Thy will be done on earth, as it is in heaven.
Give us this day our daily bread,
And forgive us our trespasses,
As we forgive those who trespass against us,
And lead us not into temptation,
But deliver us from evil.

ANGEL OF GOD/PRAYER TO ONE'S GUARDIAN ANGEL

Angel of God, my guardian dear,
To whom God's love commits me here,
Ever this day be at my side,
To light and guard, to rule and guide. Amen.

APOSTLES' CREED

I believe in God, the Father almighty,
Creator of heaven and earth,

And in Jesus Christ, his only Son, our Lord,
Who was conceived by the Holy Spirit,
Born of the Virgin Mary,
Suffered under Pontius Pilate,
Was crucified, died and was buried;
He descended into hell;
On the third day he rose again from the dead;
He ascended into heaven, and is
Seated at the right hand of God the Father almighty;
From there he will come to judge the living and the dead.
I believe in the Holy Spirit, the holy Catholic Church,
The communion of saints, the forgiveness of sins,
The resurrection of the body, and life everlasting.
Amen.

NICENE CREED

I believe in one God, the Father almighty, maker of heaven
And earth, of all things visible and invisible.
I believe in one Lord Jesus Christ, the Only Begotten Son of God,
Born of the Father before all ages.
God from God, Light from Light, true God from true God,
begotten, not made,
Consubstantial with the Father; through him all things were made.
For us men and for our salvation he came down from heaven,
And by the Holy Spirit was incarnate of the Virgin Mary, and became
man.
For our sake he was crucified under Pontius Pilate, he suffered death
And was buried, and rose again on the third day in accordance with
the Scriptures.
He ascended into heaven and is seated at the right hand of the
Father.
He will come again in glory to judge the living and the dead
And his kingdom will have no end.
I believe in the Holy Spirit, the Lord, the giver of life, who

Proceeds from the Father and the Son, who with the Father and the
Son is adored and glorified, who has spoken through the prophets.
I believe in one, holy, catholic and apostolic Church. I confess one
Baptism for the forgiveness of sins and I look forward to the
Resurrection of the dead and the life of the world to come.
Amen.

ACT OF CONTRITION

O my God, I am heartily sorry for having offended Thee,
And I detest all my sins because of thy just punishments,
But most of all because they offend Thee, my God,
Who art all good and deserving of all my love.
I firmly resolve with the help of Thy grace to sin no more
And to avoid the near occasion of sin.
Amen.

ACT OF FAITH

O my God, I firmly believe that
You are one God in three divine
Persons, Father, Son, and Holy
Spirit. I believe that your divine Son
Became man and died for our sins
And that he will come to judge the
Living and the dead. I believe these
And all the truths which the Holy
Catholic Church teaches because
You have revealed them who are
Eternal truth and wisdom, who can
Neither deceive nor be deceived. In
This faith I intend to live and die.
Amen.

ACT OF HOPE

O Lord God, I hope by your

Grace for the pardon of all my
Sins and after life here to gain
Eternal happiness because you
Have promised it who are infinitely
Powerful, faithful, kind, and
Merciful. In this hope I intend to
Live and die. Amen.

ACT OF LOVE

O Lord God, I love you above
All things and I love my neighbor
For your sake because you are the
Highest, infinite and perfect good,
Worthy of all my love. In this love I
Intend to live and die. Amen.

ANGELUS

V. The Angel of the Lord declared unto Mary.
R. And she conceived of the Holy Spirit.

Hail, Mary, full of grace, the Lord is with thee.
Blessed art thou among women
And blessed is the fruit of thy womb, Jesus.

Holy Mary, Mother of God,
Pray for us sinners,
Now and at the hour of our death.
Amen.

V. Behold the handmaid of the Lord.
R. Be it done unto me according to thy word.

Hail Mary.

V. And the Word was made flesh.
R. And dwelt among us.

Hail Mary.

V. Pray for us, O holy Mother of God.
R. That we may be made worthy of the promises of Christ.

Let us pray:
Pour forth, we beseech thee, O Lord,
Thy grace into our hearts; that we,
To whom the Incarnation of Christ, thy Son,
Was made known by the message of an angel,
May by his Passion and Cross be brought
To the glory of his Resurrection.
Through the same Christ, our Lord.
Amen.

ANIMA CHRISTI

Soul of Christ, be my sanctification.
Body of Christ, be my salvation.
Blood of Christ, fill all my veins.
Water of Christ's side, wash out my stains.
Passion of Christ, my comfort be.
O good Jesu, listen to me.
In Thy wounds I fain would hide,
Ne'er to be parted from Thy side,
Guard me, should the foe assail me.
Call me when my life shall fail me.
Bid me come to Thee above,
With Thy saints to sing Thy love,
World without end. Amen.

HAIL, HOLY QUEEN

Hail, Holy Queen, Mother of Mercy,
Our life, our sweetness and our hope.
To thee do we cry, poor banished children of Eve.
O thee do we send up our sighs,
Mourning and weeping in this valley of tears.
Turn then, most gracious advocate,
Thane eyes of mercy toward us,
And after this our exile
Show unto us the blessed fruit of thy womb, Jesus.
O clement, O loving, O sweet Virgin Mary.

Printed in Great Britain
by Amazon